WEDDING INVITATIONS

WEDDING
invitations

JENNIFER CEGIELSKI
PHOTOGRAPHS BY DANA GALLAGHER

STEWART, TABORI & CHANG · NEW YORK

Mr. and Mrs. Adam McPhee
Five Lighthouse Lane
Cape Elizabeth, Maine
04107

Mr. and Mrs. Albert Joseph Wakeman
request the honour of your presence
at the marriage of their daughter
Brittany Leigh
to
Dr. Ronald Timothy Duncan
on Saturday, the seventh of July
at half after five o'clock
Saint Luke's Church
Three South Main Street
New York City

MR. AND MRS. WILLIAM F. PARKER, JR.
AND THE PARENTS OF ERIK BERESFORD
REQUEST THE HONOUR OF YOUR PRESENCE

Dr. and Mrs. Allen Park
request the honour of your presence
at the marriage of their daughter
Rebecca Ann
to
Mr. David William Conner
on Saturday the twenty-third of May

CONTENTS

tucked among the usual contents of the mail—bills, catalogs, flyers, magazines, perhaps the odd postcard or letter—is something special. Judging by the pretty envelope, the shape, or maybe even the handwriting or return address, it is unmistakably an invitation. And though birthdays and dinner parties are fun, it's even more wonderful if the invitation occasion is something as joyous as a wedding. Now when you are the one are getting married, chances are your close friends and family know all about it long before you post the invitations. Good news travels fast! So why is it necessary to carry on the tradition of sending them?

At its most utilitarian, this document presents the facts of time and place so your guests know when and where you want them to go. On another level, it sends the message to your family and friends that they are so dear you wish

For a twist on an otherwise traditional invitation, color speaks volumes. ⟩
Tone-on-tone blues, an abstract motif, and a coordinating envelope liner modernize
this ceremony invitation, which is formally worded for a Catholic nuptial mass.

MR. AND MRS. DONALD FINDLAY

REQUEST THE HONOUR OF YOUR PRESENCE

AT THE NUPTIAL MASS UNITING THEIR DAUGHTER

Cari Natalie

AND

Mr. Daniel Harper Boylan

IN THE SACRAMENT OF HOLY MATRIMONY

SATURDAY, THE TWENTY-SIXTH OF AUGUST

TWO THOUSAND AND SIX

AT ELEVEN O'CLOCK IN THE MORNING

SAINT PATRICK'S CATHEDRAL

CHARLOTTE, NORTH CAROLINA

them to be present at one of the most meaningful events of your life. Besides, who could deny guests the pleasure of receiving a beautiful invitation in the mail? A wedding is a celebration like no other, and the invitation heralds the event and helps build the excitement leading up to it.

By sending invitations you are joining other brides and grooms in tradition throughout the ages. How did this all come to be? In order to understand the origin of wedding invitations, it is helpful to briefly look back at the evolution of the marriage event itself. It is known that a few onlookers were called to bear witness at nuptial ceremonies dating back to early Roman civilizations; in these weddings of powerful family unions or dowry-driven financial gain, witnesses were useful in case the marriage was contested. By the Middle Ages in Europe, weddings became an opportunity for extended family to celebrate kinship by following the marriage proceedings with sumptuous feasts and banquets rife with drinking and singing. These precursors of the modern wedding reception marked the beginning of the couple's new life together, once the final rites of installing the wife in her husband's home were complete. Some medieval newlyweds were subjected to having select guests present at their first bridal bed to ensure consummation (we can all breathe a sigh of relief invitations for this particular event are no longer issued).

Coincidentally, as the popularity of wedding feasts grew, so too did the ability to make paper. While Ancient Egyptians and Greeks had papyrus and parchment, we can thank the Chinese during the first century B.C. for the types of paper we know today. Over centuries, Arabs adopted Chinese techniques of papermaking and eventually introduced them to Europe where they flourished by the 1400s. We can also raise a glass to Johann Gutenberg for his little 1453 invention known as the movable type press, which paved the way for the modern methods of printing now used to create invitations.

At what point did the worlds of weddings and printed paper collide? It's a safe guess invitations first appeared somewhere between the years 1600 and 1800, when written and printed documents began to be accessible to common households and not just royalty and the clergy. And while it is difficult to pinpoint the happy couple who first made the request for guests with a printed invitation, the concept could possibly be derived from the wording of wedding charters created in feudal France. Wedding charters were pieces of paper detailing the ceremony, the names of the bride and groom, and the date of the wedding. Along with a ring, the new wife received a charter from her husband as a wedding souvenir. Much later, printed wedding announcements came into vogue, and the strict behavior codes of the Victorian era begat the social etiquette that governs wedding invitations of today.

All this history aside, if you are planning a wedding the selection of your invitation is an important step as the invitation sets the stage for the event for your guests and directs the look and feel of many other elements of the day. Know too that not only are you providing guests with the details and giving them a hint of what to expect, you are making a bold and very public first statement about who you are as a couple. What will your invitation say about the two of you? ❧

1

GETTING STARTED

although it might be tempting soon after you've gotten engaged to start thinking about how your two names will look together on paper, you'll need to make certain wedding decisions before you are ready to choose your invitations. In a nutshell you will have to envision the event, from its overall style to its size to its season, in order to create an invitation that is right for your wedding. Made your guest list? Check. Picked a date? Got it. Next, you will have made arrangements for your ceremony site and booked your officiant as well as your reception site. Once you have crossed these related tasks off your to-do list, you can begin to create your perfect wedding invitation.

page 10 Together, your names can serve as a sort of logo for your invitation as well as other wedding paper goods like program covers, favor boxes, and thank you cards.

your wedding style

There are hundreds if not thousands of styles of wedding invitations to pore through. The design you choose should be consistent with the look and feel of the wedding you have planned to help clue your guests in to what the event will be like. Guests will also be able to infer what they should wear from the style of your invitation, learn the time of day of the event, and its location. Collecting your thoughts on the formality, personal style, and individual details of your wedding early on will help you focus when it comes to sifting through your invitation options later.

FORMALITY   One easy way to immediately narrow down the range is to think about the level of formality for your particular wedding. Invitations can convey formality through selection of paper, printing method, type style, and wording. A very formal white- or black-tie affair certainly calls for the most classic invitation, as does a wedding where the ceremony is steeped in religious tradition. This generally translates into white or ecru paper engraved or printed with a formal lettering style. A semi-formal wedding gives you a little more freedom—you might make use of formal wording, but lighten the sentiment with colored paper or a themed motif. For informal nuptials on a beach or in a garden, private home or restaurant, you could make a casual statement with a handwritten invitation or a simple design you've printed from your own computer.

anna and james
together with their families
invite you to celebrate
their marriage

march 6th, 2003
at 4 o'clock

hollyhock house
andover, new jersey

cocktail reception
to follow

rsvp 201 792 0581

anna blum and james nies
782 garden street
hoboken, new jersey 07030

PERSONAL STYLE At your very core, how would you describe your-selves? Whether you're traditionalists or minimalists, stick with your own style for your wedding and your invitations. For example, it only makes sense to choose traditional bells and whistles like tissue inserts and lined envelopes if you generally take a classic approach to most other parts of your life. If you live by a more carefree philosophy, unfettered by the trappings of conven-tion, by all means express yourself through your choices. The best invitations are the ones where guests have an idea of who is getting married before they even read the names.

INDIVIDUAL DETAILS Of course every wedding is unique, so don't pass up the opportunity to capitalize on the details of your own for a truly special invitation. Your invitation is the ideal place to debut a theme if you have one. Or, take a cue from your location to establish a motif—if you're returning to your hometown to wed, a local landmark might be a fitting emblem. Likewise, if you are wedding on the waterfront, something beach related or nautical could do the trick. Seasons are also ripe with symbols and imagery. Autumn's falling leaves, winter's snowflakes, spring's trees and flowers, and summer's sun can all be used to beautiful effect. If you have been inspired by a favorite color, make the most of it with your choice of paper, ink, or borders.

your limits

What would your wedding and invitation be like if you had all the time in the world to plan, an endless guest list, and a bottomless budget? Now take

< This boldly colored example is designed with contemporary wording that acknowledges both families and offers a telephone number in lieu of a traditional reply card.

SAVE-THE-DATE CARDS

A trend over the past several years, save-the-date cards plant the seed for your wedding in guests' minds before they ever receive your official invitation. Think of them as the hors d'oeuvres before the appetizer. These cards are particularly useful for getting on your loved ones' calendars early, especially important for destination weddings, weddings around a holiday, or weddings where the majority of guests will be traveling and need to make air and accommodations reservations.

WHAT THEY ARE A save-the-date card can be as simple as a postcard or as complex as a little packet filled with travel details, maps, and sightseeing brochures. Essential information to include: your names and the date and location of your wedding (city and state); if you've blocked out hotel rooms or arranged for special rates you can mention this too.

WHEN TO SEND About six months prior to the wedding, or even up to a year before if your wedding is near or on a major holiday or requires extended travel.

IDEAS a strip of funny photobooth photos with the info written on the back, a refrigerator magnet printed with the details, a mini calendar with your date circled and information attached, or a postcard from the destination.

into account your actual resources. Be aware of what your limits are and remember to live within them when choosing your invitation.

GUEST LIST Composing the guest list often becomes one of the most infamously laborious tasks of wedding planning, but without it you can't move forward on many of your other decisions, including invitations. The list is ultimately composed of a combination of any of the following: your friends

A charming calendar save-the-date card might make its way onto a guest's > bulletin board. Offering as much information as possible ahead of time on the reverse helps guests solidify their travel plans for faraway affairs.

october

		1	2	3	4
5	6	7	8	9	10	11
12	13	14	15	16	17	(18)
19	20	21	22	23	24	25
26	27	28	29	30	31

to have and to hold from this day forward

E & CORD

kindly save the date

Wedding Day Details

Anne Reichardt and Cord Shiflet will say "I Do!" at Barton Creek Country Club
in Austin, Texas on Saturday, October 18, 2003 at 5:30 in the evening.
The reception will immediately follow.

Where to Stay

Rooms will be blocked at the following locations (all reserved under Reichardt/Shiflet):

Barton Creek Resort and Conference Center
8212 Barton Club Drive, Austin, TX 78735
(800) 336-6158, www.bartoncreek.com
$200/night (ceremony and reception site)

La Quinta Inn
4525 Gaines Ranch Loop, Austin, TX 78735
(800) 531-5900, www.lq.com
$95-105/night (4.3 miles from Barton Creek)

(512)457-8800, www.intercontinental.com
$169/night (7.5 miles from Barton Creek)

Questions?

We hope to see you there! If you have any questions, please contact
Anne at anner@austin.rr.com or Cord at cord@moreland.com.

10.18.03
ANNE & CORD

Invitation to follow

and colleagues, close family, extended family, and parents' wish lists on both sides. The number of invitations are more or less divided equally among the different camps, but it is customary to denote more if a particular party is contributing more to the wedding coffers. It is usually helpful to establish an "A" list of must-have guests and a "B" list of additional people whom you'd love to have there but can live without if absolutely necessary. The guest list ultimately impacts your other two important limits, time and money.

TIME In general, you'll need plenty of time to search for or create your invitation, then enough time to proofread the final selection and print the number needed. Most wedding planning experts clock this span at about six to eight months, from conception to completion. Consider further that the longer the guest list the longer it will take to assemble and address the invitations, so be sure to build some extra time into your planning schedule if you have a large list. In addition, if you've contemplated the idea of making your invitations yourself there is obviously a big difference between a guest list numbering seventy-five and one over two hundred. Be honest with yourself and decide whether or not you are up to such an undertaking and how much time you'll realistically have to devote to the task.

BUDGET The typical couple spends between two and five percent of their overall wedding budget on invitations, with the total cost spread across invitations and printing, envelope addressing, calligraphy, and postage. Depending on the design and certain aspects of the quality, invitation prices can be as economical as a dollar to upwards of thirty dollars a piece. The good news is, with so many available options there is a match for every wedding, though expensive handmade invitations or costly extras like hand-sewn edges or appliques might be out of the question for truly large guest lists. Likewise, invitations with several enclosures such as maps and travel information might not be fiscally possible for larger invite lists. If you have your heart set on an oversized or irregular shape, don't forget to take into account the additional money that will need to be spent on extra postage. Also calligraphers charge by the piece or by the line to address your envelopes, so again the size of your guest list makes a difference.

your inspiration

If you're ready to start collecting ideas, begin by talking to married friends about where they got their invitations. You can also visit stationery stores for inspiration or make appointments to review their custom-ordered wedding offerings. Wedding magazines and books, of course, are great resources to flip through. You'll find invitation information through online wedding resources, and there are now many online invitation companies and stationers with a wide variety of designs to browse. Many of these online resources offer interactive tools where you can experiment with wording or see what your information would look like on different backgrounds. If you are interested in creating your own invitations, arrange some time to meet with a graphic designer or independent printer to explore your options. Start an inspiration file with paper swatches, actual invitation samples, favorite type style examples, clip art you find appealing, tear sheets from magazines, and the like. You'll start to see your style emerge through the various elements you collect, and however you ultimately obtain your invitations you'll be able to refer back to your ideas again and again.

Mr. and Mrs. Clifford Alan Curtis
request the honour of your presence
at the marriage of their daughter

NATHALIE VAUGHN
to
MR. STUART CHRISTOPHER PIERSON

❧

Saturday, the eighteenth of September
at four o'clock
Holy Ghost Church
Denver, Colorado

KINDLY REPLY
before the fourth of September

Mr. and Mrs. Clifford Alan Curtis
28 Knoll Crest Circle
Cherry Hills Village, Colorado 80111

RECEPTION

❧

immediately following the ceremony
Grand Ballroom
The Oxford Hotel

2

ELEMENTS

the simple word "invitation" is somewhat misleading for a wedding invitation is often more than just a single card or piece of paper. An invitation set or ensemble, as they are called, might include the main invitation, a separate card with reception or ceremony specifics, some form of reply card for guests to post back, and an envelope or two, not to mention assorted enclosures bearing various bits of information regarding anything from special seating to travel arrangements. For presentation's sake, all of these elements are generally printed in a coordinating style using the same method, paper, type, and ink color. Each item is not always essential for every wedding, and your individual needs will be the driving force behind determining exactly which of these pieces are required. To help you decide, keep in mind whether you plan on inviting your entire guest list to both the ceremony and the reception, and whether you will need to provide anything beyond the invitation basics such as maps or admission tickets. You'll find wording examples for these elements starting on page 148.

page 20 A classic ensemble includes a ceremony invitation, a reception card, and a reply card and envelope. This square format is an elegant alternative to the standard rectangle.

the invitation itself

Let's start with the veritable star of the show—the wedding invitation. All the vital details of the event are communicated here, including the names of the two people getting married as well as the facts as to when, where, and what time. Most traditionally, the formal invitation is designed as a flat, single-panel rectangular card or a folded medium-weight paper. Modern interpretations have evolved and now include invitations in different shapes such as square or round, or even interesting foldout or accordion styles. You'll find more on what your options are in the next chapter. Regardless of what physical style of invitation you ultimately decide to create or how you choose to word it, remember the essential information should be clear and to the point. Specifically, there are three main formats of wedding invitations.

CEREMONY INVITATION The most common in use as well as the most formal in style, the ceremony invitation conveys only the particulars regarding the rite or service uniting the couple. With this option, guests invited to a reception would also receive a reception card with an "R.s.v.p." request, or separate reception and response cards.

CEREMONY AND RECEPTION INVITATION This combination invitation requests guests' presence to both the union as well as to any festivities afterwards. It is used when the wedding is semi-formal or informal and all the guests for the ceremony are also invited to the reception. For this type, it is best when the two events occur at the same location, but it may be used when they are in different places provided that the wording is not too long or too complicated and won't dominate the overall invitation. Either the use of "R.s.v.p" on the invitation or a separate response card is appropriate.

RECEPTION INVITATION A third type extends the invitation to the wedding reception only. This is the choice when the ceremony will be small and private or held at a courthouse, and the majority of the guests will only take part in the party. Either the use of "R.s.v.p" on the invitation or a separate response card would be appropriate in this instance as well.

the reception card

Designed to accompany a ceremony invitation, this additional card communicates where (name and address) and when the reception (or breakfast, cocktail party, etc.) will be held. Generally it is smaller in size than the invitation. A reception card may also be used for semi-formal or informal weddings when the ceremony and reception are held in the same location if all of the pertaining information will not fit on the main invitation. However, formal invitations always use a separate reception card. If you are not including a response card with your overall invitation, you may indicate "R.s.v.p." on the reception card.

the ceremony card

This smaller-sized card is designed to accompany a reception invitation and communicates to the select invited guests where and when the ceremony will take place. If the guest list for the ceremony is very small, this card may be handwritten instead of printed for a personal—as well as cost-effective—touch.

the response card and envelope

Although the act of sending an invitation is gracious, it's the potential guests' responses that make or break your celebration. Wedding etiquette of years past instructed that invitations be discreetly printed with "R.s.v.p.", an abbreviation for the French *Répondez s'il vous plaît* meaning "please reply," and guests would respond in kind with a handwritten note or letter on their own stationery.

In twenty-first century times, realism prevails and response cards have come into fashion for eliciting a "yes" or "no" from invitees. Tucked in the envelope along with the invitation and reception card, this thoughtful enclosure makes it easy for your guests to respond and helps ensure that you actually receive a response. Responses are important; your budget and headcount depend on them. A traditional response card is a single flat card with an addressed, stamped envelope. To save on paper and postage, couples holding semi-formal or informal weddings may provide a simple addressed and stamped postcard for responses.

traditional enclosures

Depending on the special instances of your wedding, there are a few traditional enclosures that you might include in your invitation. Often, these enclosures deal with special admission or seating and are brought by the guests to the wedding. They are smaller in scale than the invitation itself, and usually pocket-sized.

ADMISSION CARDS Consider these cards tickets that guarantee only your guests attend your wedding. They are usually provided when the

The marriage of
Ann Marie Mortimer
and
Michael Kirst

21 September 200

CEREMONY PROGRAMS

Every great performance deserves a program, and getting married is no exception. While not mandatory, these guides are sweet extras that make lovely keepsakes. Programs offer a who's who of those involved and map out the ceremony to help guests follow along as you are wed. They are not bound by the same rules of etiquette as invitations, so feel free to be as creative as you like. You might tie them in some way to your invitations, but stylistically they can be as simple as a folded sheet of paper you've designed on your computer or as elaborate as a ribbon-bound booklet with a cardstock cover you've had professionally printed.

STANDARD INFORMATION
Your names
The date
The location
Chronologic ceremony outline
Titles of readings and songs
Name of officiant
Names of wedding party members and their relation to the couple
Names of others involved (readers, soloists, etc.)

PERSONAL FLOURISHES
Dedications and thanks
Words to readings, songs, or vows
Foreign translations
Explanations of cultural or religious traditions
Favorite poem or quote
Meaningful motif or monogram
A current or vintage photograph

< If you prepare in advance, elements like program covers may be printed at the same time as your invitations. Here, a monogram incorporating first initials of the bride and groom is a unifying motif.

REHEARSAL DINNER INVITATIONS

Your wedding may not be the only event deserving an invitation. It is customary in the days preceeding the wedding for the groom's family to host a dinner (or brunch, lunch, etc.) following the rehearsal of the wedding ceremony. While a simple telephone call or handwritten note might convey the invitation for an intimate celebration, a very large or formal event requires a more official printed announcement with an "R.s.v.p.".

WHO GETS ONE For a traditional rehearsal dinner, parents and immediate family members, wedding party participants and their significant others, children in the wedding and their parents, other friends and family with tasks such as reading or singing, perhaps your officiant if you feel you have a close relationship with him or her. Some couples decide to have a more informal rehearsal dinner and extend the invitation to out-of-town guests and others not involved in the wedding party.

WHEN TO SEND Three to four weeks prior to the wedding.

ceremony or reception takes place in a location open to the general public or at a members-only private club, or when people involved in the wedding or invited guests are well known and there is concern about party crashers or gawkers at the event. It should be clear from the wording that these cards are to be brought to the wedding for admission. See the Appendix on page 138 for examples of how to word these cards.

RESERVED SEATING CARDS If you are inviting a very large number of guests or your ceremony space is limited, you'll want to make sure VIPs like your parents, grandparents, and other special relatives and friends get priority seating. Guests present reserved seating cards to your ushers upon arrival at the ceremony. Although not essential, these little cards will direct the ushers to seat these individuals accordingly. Pew cards indicate a specific pew or row where you wish the person to be seated. "Within the ribbon" cards are used when you have cordoned off a series of rows with ribbon or cording along the aisle to make a special section, but aren't concerned with specific assigned rows.

"AT HOME" CARDS Although a somewhat old-fashioned custom, these optional cards notify your near and dear of what your newlywed address will be and as of what date you will be in residence. At home cards can also indicate whether the bride will be taking her husband's last name or retaining her maiden name. Traditionally the cards are included in the invitation, but you may send them after the wedding if you prefer.

informative enclosures

One reality of modern day matrimony is the fact that many couples do not necessarily meet and marry in their hometowns anymore. They may decide to wed in the city where they now reside, at a location equidistant from both of their families, or even in a separate city which resonates with meaning for them. As a result, a good number of guests travel in from out of town to attend a wedding and may be unfamiliar with the area as well as the locations of the ceremony and reception. Or, similarly, you may be planning a wedding at a far-flung destination where everyone will be traveling to attend. If either of these scenarios is the case for your wedding, it is customary to include informative enclosures corresponding to airlines and hotels, maps and directions, or parking information and prearranged transportation. Your guests will appreciate the gesture, and you'll rest easier knowing you've done everything you can to make sure everyone knows how to get where they are going. For the most elegant presentation, the printing of all informative enclosures should also match your invitations, though you may use a simpler type style. If printing these enclosures in the same way as your invitations is cost-prohibitive or if you wish to preserve the sanctity of your invitation, you can always print them on your computer and send them under separate cover once you have received a guest's response. You need only send travel- or direction-related enclosures to out-of-town guests.

TRAVEL AND ACCOMODATIONS If you have secured a special airline rate for your guests, have chartered a flight, or there are limited airlines flying to your wedding site and you recommend guests book early you can communicate that here. You may also let guests know about any hotel rooms you have blocked out at special rates, or you can provide a short list of nearby hotels and their phone numbers and internet addresses for guests to inquire themselves.

MAPS AND DRIVING DIRECTIONS These tools are critical to help guests get from point A to point B with the least amount of homework and headache on their part. A map may be beautifully drawn by hand or reproduced from a larger map or atlas. Be sure to include major roads and applicable landmarks. Any written directions you provide are best in simple step-by-step instructions, and it is helpful if you offer at least two main points of orientation (for example, coming from the north and coming from the south). Internet mapping sites are a good source for establishing directions, but always make sure to double check each step in person (or delegate someone to do so for you) in case there are any road changes or detours in effect. If you do include maps and directions, you do not need to print an address for your ceremony and reception on the invitation or accompanying reception or ceremony cards. However, if the two events are in different locations, you may wish to have extra copies of the directions on hand at the ceremony for guests to take as they head from one site to the other.

PARKING AND TRANSPOR-TATION When many of your guests will be driving, it is thoughtful to include a card indicating where the nearest parking lots are and whether or not there will be valet service (usually complimentary with gratuities prepaid by the bride and groom). Some couples even go so far as to provide transportation for their guests; if you do, be sure to let guests know prior to the wedding so they don't book their own unnecessarily, and outline when and where they need to be to board the boat, bus, trolley, train, or sleigh. See the Appendix on page 138 for examples of how to word these cards especially if you intend the enclosure card to serve as a parking pass or ticket to board the provided transportation.

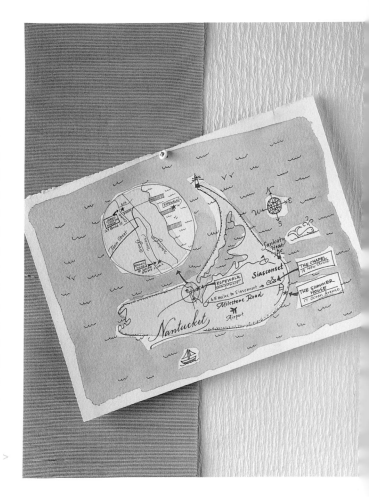

A hand-drawn map need not be to scale—simply include a few landmarks and major roads. This map was also hand-colored and makes a lovely keepsake.

Once you've figured out your invitation requirements, pause for a moment and think ahead to how your reception will progress. When guests arrive, how will they know which table to go to? How will they know where to sit? To complete your wedding stationery ensemble, consider any paper aides needed for seating, table identification, and menu communication. Whether you produce your reception stationery yourself or have it printed by the same source as your invitations, you might like to incorporate any motif or theme carried throughout the rest of your wedding. All of these elements may either be printed, calligraphed, or hand-written.

ESCORT CARDS Also known as seating cards, these stationery snippets greet your guests near the entrance of the reception (usually set up alphabetically by last name on a special table). Traditionally single cards in little envelopes or tented cards, the cards direct guests to the particular tables where they will be seated. Less formally, you may choose to place the cards within little frames for guests to keep or do something creative, such as making the escort cards paper leaves and tying them to branches arranged in urns. The card or envelope should have the guest's name written on it, as well as a table number or table name identified.

TABLE CARDS Once guests have an escort card, they enter the reception and look for their table, which is identified by a table card. Standard table cards are

ITINERARY   With the rise in the number of out-of-town wedding guests, it has also become popular for brides and grooms to extend the celebration over the course of a few days or over the weekend in order to spend more time with their loved ones. Activities such as welcome lunches, open rehearsal dinners, golf outings, family softball games, sightseeing trips, or goodbye brunches might be planned. A printed itinerary is a lovely way to kick off these festivities, and also gives guests the opportunity to book their numbered, but for a more creative spin give your tables names—such as all the destinations you've travelled to together or will visit on your honeymoon, landmark names based on the location of your wedding, names derived from your wedding theme (for example, different types of trees if your invitation has a leaf or tree motif), or other meaningful monikers. Display flat table cards on a small stand or in a frame, and keep their presence visible but subtle.

MENU CARDS While not essential, menu cards are an elegant token. The different courses for the meal are presented, and the cards are either placed at each place setting or displayed two or three to a table.

PLACE CARDS While some couples may simply use assigned table cards and allow guests to choose their own seats once there, these cards are set up at each place setting to designate specific seats. Traditional place cards are flat or tented, while less formal interpretations might be a pretty piece of paper with the guest's name on it tacked to a small decorative fruit or a party favor to double as a keepsake.

SIGNAGE Depending on the needs of your site, it might be helpful to have some signs prepared to stylishly declare "No Smoking, Please", "Please add your bit of wedding wisdom to our guest book," or "We invite you to take a favor home with you" or other similar messages.

travel plans accordingly. This is another item you may choose to send with the invitation or separately once you have received a guest's response.

ALTERNATE PLANS Occasionally a couple will choose to get married in a location prone to inclement weather. For example, an outdoor garden wedding in the middle of a wet spring, a beach wedding on the cusp of tropical storm season, or a mountain-top wedding in an area occasionally hit by blizzards might call for back up plans. While your own situation might not be so dramatic, if you are concerned about the impact of rain, wind, or snow upon your affair you can inform guests of an alternate site on a separate card.

the envelopes

Truly traditional invitation ensembles are packaged in two envelopes—an outer envelope for mailing with an enclosed inner envelope holding all the contents. This custom dates back to the days when invitations were delivered by hand. The soiled outer envelope would be removed by the servants, and the mistress of the house would receive the invitation in the spotless inner envelope.

THE INNER ENVELOPE Though no longer considered absolutely essential, the inner envelope is still used for formal invitations or by those who have a multitude of enclosures or wish to heighten the surprise of what's inside. Couples looking to save paper or money can certainly opt out of using an inner envelope. This envelope's purpose is to protect the invitation, response card, and any enclosures. For decoration, the inner envelope may be lined in a coordinating paper. It is not gummed and is left unsealed, and no return address on the back flap is necessary. Inner envelopes are addressed more simply than outer envelopes; turn to page 150 for examples.

THE OUTER ENVELOPE The larger of the two envelopes, the outer version has a return address printed on the back flap. Your guest's title, full name and address are written (usually in handwriting or calligraphy) on the front; see page 48 for a guide to addressing your envelopes. Once everything is safely tucked away inside and the envelope has been addressed, you stamp it and mail it; see chapter six for more about this part of the process.

When you know the guests intimately, the inner envelope >
may be written more personally with first names.

MR. AND MRS. JOHN GRAFF

REQUEST THE HONOUR OF YOUR PRESENCE

AT THE MARRIAGE OF THEIR DAUGHTER

Julie Kathryn

TO

Stephen James Plzak

SON OF DR. LOUIS PLZAK, JR. AND MRS. JUDITH PLZAK

ON SATURDAY, THE TWENTY-NINTH OF NOVEMBER

TWO THOUSAND AND THREE

AT TWO O'CLOCK IN THE AFTERNOON

SAINTS PETER AND PAUL CHURCH

WEST CHESTER, PENNSYLVANIA

3

ETIQUETTE

these days, most of us no longer have the time—nor the inclination—to seriously memorize etiquette manuals to learn rules on how to live our lives. Edicts such as whether a man should guide a woman by the elbow when they are walking down the street seem almost quaintly out of date and have little to do with most people's everyday lives. That being said, there is an established etiquette for wedding invitations and it is worth following. Designed to communicate various bits of information (both directly and subtly) surrounding the wedding, this specific etiquette extends to the wording on the invitation as well as the wording on the envelopes and response card. Etiquette also offers guidance with regards to the timing for the sending of invitations, and, thankfully, etiquette can also help you address any sticky situations that may arise with your guests. Luckily none of this is as complicated as you may think.

page 36 Many couples these days are finding it a thoughtful gesture to include a mention of the groom's parents on the invitation even when the bride's parents are the hosts.

traditional invitation wording

Whether your wedding is formal or informal, the formulaic code of wedding invitations conveys to your guests what they need to know in a style befitting the significance of the event. An invitation may be issued to invite loved ones to your marriage ceremony, to the reception only if the ceremony is small and private, or to both the ceremony and reception. In all three instances, each line plays a part in announcing who, what, when and where. The examples here generally follow traditional formal etiquette; as with everything relative to the wedding, this wording may be adjusted to the formality of the event and the sentiments and style of the couple.

THE HOST LINE   The very first line is known as the host line, and it is written in the third person. Historically speaking, the names that most commonly appear in this spot are those of the bride's parents. This hearkens back to marriage contracts of medieval days when a bride was "given" by her father to the groom who "took" her for his wife, and the bride went directly from living with her parents to living with her husband. As we all know, times mercifully have changed and couples now have several options for who gets top billing on their invitations. Technically, this line should be the name or names of the hosts of the wedding. There is some debate as to whether host really implies financial sponsor; the choice is yours. Some couples continue to list the bride's parents as the hosts, while some couples prefer to have the invitation issued by both sets of parents to be more inclusive and avoid hard feelings. Still others choose to issue the invitations themselves, particularly if they are getting married later in life. One very modern and newly acceptable way to combine these concepts is to have the bride and groom issue the invitation and add the words "together with their families." In addition, contemporary family structures—divorces, remarriages, retained maiden names— may make wording even more intricate when it comes to naming names. Regardless of what your personal family situation is, there's a way to word it on an invitation. You'll find examples of the many permutations in the Appendix on page 139.

THE REQUEST LINE The second line is where the actual "inviting" takes place. The phrase "request the honour of your presence" specifically serves the solemnity of ceremonies held in a house of worship, while the lighter "request the pleasure of your company" is preferred for a ceremony at a restaurant, hotel, or home or on an invitation to a reception only. Note that the deferential "honour" is usually spelled English-style with the addition of "u." For a less-traditional affair, a bride and groom issuing the invitation may "invite you to share in their love and future together" or "invite you to celebrate their marriage."

THE EVENT LINE Here what the guests are being invited to is outlined. For example, in the case of the bride's parents issuing the invitation, this line may read "at the marriage of their daughter" for the ceremony, or "at the wedding reception for their daughter" for a reception invitation. When both sets of parents are hosting, this line may read "at the marriage of their children." If the couple is issuing the invitation, this line could simply be worded "at their marriage" or "at their wedding reception." When the invitation is for both the ceremony and reception together, the wording follows the ceremony format, and mention of the reception is at the end of the invitation (see page 147 for an example of this).

THE BRIDE AND GROOM LINES In these lines, the bride- and groom-to-be are named individually with the woman's name always preceding the man's. For traditional invitations issued by the bride's parents, their daughter would be referred to by her first and middle names, with no title or last name, and the joining word "to" for the ceremony or "and" for the reception only would be used. "And" would also be used if both sets of parents are issuing. If the couple is issuing their own invitations, they would use their titles of Miss (or Ms.) and Mr. as well as their last names and the joining word "and." The groom is referred to by his full name (first, middle, and last) and his title (Mr., Doctor, and so on; see page 42 for proper use of titles) may also be used on the most formal of invitations. Initials and nicknames should not be used in place of any proper names.

THE DATE AND YEAR LINES Quite possibly, these lines convey the most critical information. For formal invitations, everything is written out in full, the day of the week is capitalized, and no numerals are used. On one line is the day, the date, and the month, i.e. "Sunday, the twentieth of May." Including the year is optional (guests will assume you are referring to the next available twentieth of May), but if you choose to include it it should appear on the following line, i.e. "two thousand and eight." You may choose to include or skip the word "on" prior to the day of the week, and for casual weddings using the numerals for the year is certainly acceptable.

THE TIME LINE Next is the time of day, also written out in full for formal invitations, i.e. "three o'clock" or "half after two o'clock." The use of AM or PM is not necessary, however if you are concerned your timing might

TITLES

For the parents of both the bride and groom, titles of "Mr." and "Mrs." should always be used and are the only acceptable abbrieviations on the invitation. The father's given and middle names are used in conjunction with the titles, i.e. "Mr. and Mrs. Albert Reeves Cook." Alternatively, if any of the parents have a professional title, this may be used instead and should be spelled out. These titles include:

Doctor (when a physician, not a Ph.D)

Reverend, Rabbi

The Honorable (for federal judges, governors, ambassadors, senators, congress members, cabinet members, or mayors)

Appropriate titles should also be used for those in the military

Traditionally, the bride is listed only by her given and middle name with no title or last name; however, many modern brides are now choosing to use their professional titles as well. It is optional for the groom to have Mr. or his professional title preceding his given name, middle name and last name. When the couple is issuing the invitation themselves, it is standard to use "Miss" and "Mr." However, as a general rule, whatever you choose to do for the bride's name, be consistent with the groom's name as well. In addition, it is acceptable to use "junior" spelled out and lower case; if the man's name is exceptionally long, junior may be abbrieviated to "Jr." (note the capital J). Gentlemen have the option of including "II" or "III" after their names, (with or without a comma, if applicable).

be confusing to some of your guests, say eight or nine o'clock, you can add the phrase "in the morning," "in the afternoon," or "in the evening." You may choose to precede the time with the word "at" if you like. If your wedding is on a beach or in a backyard, you might wish to simply use numerals for the time in keeping with the lighter tone of your event. Know that the time of day of your wedding communicates to your guests the level of formality of the event, for example, a six o'clock wedding indicates a formal affair.

THE LOCATION LINE   Where have you chosen your event to take place? Spell out the entire name in full here, i.e. "Saint Mary's Church," "Oak Hills Bath and Tennis Club," or "Armstrong Band Shell, Hazelton Park." Be sure to confirm the proper name of your location ("Church of Saint John the Baptist" versus "Saint John the Baptist Church") to avoid confusion for your guests. If your wedding is taking place at a private home, state "at the residence of Mr. and Mrs. Andrew Williams"; if it is taking place at the home of the issuers of the invitation, skip the location line and go directly to the address line.

THE ADDRESS AND CITY AND STATE LINES Including the actual street address is optional unless there are similarly named locations in town or there are a number of out-of-town guests who may not be familiar with the location. The address should be written in full and numerals under 100 should be spelled out, i.e. "Thirty-two Chestnut Street" or "310 West Eleventh Street." The city and state appear on a separate line and are also written out in full, i.e. "Riverside, Illinois"; for well-known cities like New York or Los Angeles, the state may be omitted.

THE RECEPTION LINE   Reception information appears next if the wedding is semi-formal or casual and all guests for the ceremony are also invited to the reception. If the ceremony and reception are in the same location, you may use the words "and afterwards at the reception" or "reception immediately following" here. Be sure to include the time if the reception is not immediately after the ceremony. When the reception is at another location, state the type of reception and where on separate lines, i.e.

at 3 o'clock

reception to follow

The Pershing Hall

reception to follow

"Cocktail Reception The Drake Hotel" or "Buffet Dinner San Lorenzo Restaurant." You may also insert the phrase "reception to follow." If the reception information is complicated (such as a long name or address), it's best to provide a separate reception card even if all guests to the ceremony are invited to the reception. Very formal weddings should always have reception information on a separate reception card.

ADDITIONAL INFORMATION AND RSVP REQUEST LINE Certain optional information may appear in the lower left-hand corner of the invitation. Often special directives such as "Black Tie" are sometimes communicated here, but this is not considered correct in terms of strict etiquette. You may wish to relay the desire for a response on a reception only invitation or ceremony and reception invitation with a phrase such as "The favour of a reply is requested," "Kindly Respond," or "Regrets Only" with an accompanying name and address; in traditional etiquette, this implies your guests should send a written reply and you should not include a response card.

envelope wording

Traditional etiquette recommends that formal wedding invitation envelopes be addressed by hand, in blue or black ink. Of course for semi-formal and casual weddings you may choose whatever ink color you wish, maybe in a hue complementing your invitations. Computer-generated labels and envelopes sent directly through a home printer are technically not considered acceptable, though some wedding experts say they may be used if they are in a calligraphy style. In general, most of the same technical rules that

< If all of your guests are invited to both the ceremony and reception and space permits, you may combine this information on the main invitation and omit a second card for informal and semi-formal weddings.

SPECIAL CONCERNS

In certain circumstances a bride and groom may heed religious or ethnic traditions. Be sure to review your wording with your officiant if you think there are potential issues or aren't sure about appropriate wording. Also, if you plan on wording your invitation in your native language but are also expecting English-speaking guests at your wedding, you may offer the English translation on the invitation as well.

HISPANIC WEDDINGS Formally, both sets of parents issue a wedding invitation, either together on one page or as a two-page invitation with wording from the bride's parents on the left side and wording from the groom's parents on the right side. When the invitation is on one page, the names of the parents each appear on their own line; first the bride's parents are listed separately, then the groom's.

JEWISH WEDDINGS With the belief that couples are joined together in marriage (as opposed to the woman joined to the man), the word "and" is employed instead of "to" in between the names of the bride and groom on an invitation to a Jewish wedding. As the two families are united the names of both sets of parents appear, either together at the top or leading with the bride's parents and ending on the groom's

apply to the invitation (no nicknames or initials, write out full address, etc.) also apply to the envelopes.

OUTER ENVELOPES These mailing envelopes are addressed on the front with guests' titles, given names, and surnames. For very formal invitations, you may include middle names as well if you know them. It should go without saying, but both partners of a married couple, engaged couple, or couple living together should be invited. For married and cohabitating couples with different surnames, the woman is always listed first. Single women may be given the title of Miss or Ms., though it is preferable to use Ms. for a divorced woman. In strictest etiquette of days past, if a woman had a title it was parents on the line after their son's name (i.e. "son of Mr. and Mrs. Ira Bernstein"). If the couple chooses wording in both Hebrew and English, the Hebrew appears on the left side of a two-page invitation and the English on the right.

MORMON WEDDINGS   Mormon ceremonies are generally small and private, so the main invitation is issued for the reception with a ceremony card provided for included close family and friends. Both sets of parents' names appear on the invitation (similar to invitations to Jewish weddings). Where and when the ceremony took place is mentioned, as is a set time period for the reception for guests to drop in briefly and offer their wishes to the couple.

ROMAN CATHOLIC WEDDINGS   If the wedding is to be performed as a Nuptial Mass (the ceremony is part of a mass service as opposed to a simple wedding service), this fact is mentioned on the invitation ("...request the honour of your presence at the Nuptial Mass uniting their daughter...") to give guests a better sense of the duration of the ceremony, which would be longer. "And" is the preferred joining word, since the couple is joined together in holy matrimony.

generally ignored and she was referred to as Miss or Mrs.; most modern couples elect for more equal treatment in their wording. If you are inviting adult men and women who reside at the same address but are not romantically involved, each should receive his or her own invitation. For some examples for outside envelopes (when inner envelopes are also used) turn to page 150.

For the mailing address, the street number or name and direction (West, North, etc.), city, and state are spelled out in full; words like Street, Avenue, Drive, Boulevard, Apartment, Post Office Box, and Rural Route are also spelled out. Most formally, numbers under one hundred are spelled out but this is not necessary for more casual weddings.

A return address (sans names) should appear on the back flap of the outside envelope. Most formally this address is that of the invitation issuer, though now some couples choose to put the address to which they would like gifts to be sent. The return address is bound by the same rules as the mailing address with regards to spelling out all pertinent information.

INNER ENVELOPES These protective envelopes are addressed slightly less formally, with only the names of the guests and no address. You may refer in a familiar way to close family, such as "Grandma" or "Uncle Phil and Aunt Kate," and nicknames may be used. The inner envelope is where you make your wishes regarding your guests' children and escorts known. To invite children under 18 years of age, write their names (as well as their parents') on the inner envelope of the parents' invitation. Not including children's names on the inner envelope is an indication to the parents that children are not invited to the wedding. The same philosophy applies to single guests and their dates or escorts; if you are allowing your guest to bring someone along, write "and Guest" following his or her name on the inner envelope. Not doing so indicates you expect your guest to attend solo. However, if you are inviting a single guest whom you know has a longtime partner, make an effort to find out that person's name and include it with your guest's on the inner envelope in lieu of using the somewhat cold "and Guest" phrasing. See page 150 examples of inner envelope wording.

response wording

As mentioned previously, formal invitations following the strictest etiquette would feature some indication of the request for a reply on the invitation itself. However, if you would prefer to include response, or reply, cards to better your chances of receiving replies, you have a few options for how to word them.

RESPONSE CARDS At the very least, a formal response card should say, "The favour of a reply is requested" with blank space for your guest to write his or her response before returning the card in the mail. The majority of response cards are a little more specific and include your request for a response and lined space for guest names and response. In former times, it was expected that genteel folk would know the correct amount of time within which to respond; these days, this knowledge has often fallen by the wayside and with caterers and reception sites imposing headcount deadlines, most couples do opt to include a response due date. See page 148 for common ways to word a response card.

∧
A standard response card issues a deadline and provides space for the guest's name as well as some indication of whether or not he or she will be attending. If you like, encourage guests to scribe something on the back—a wedding wish or marriage advice—for posterity.

The response date is generally set two weeks before the wedding date. Guests will fill in the "M_____" area with their names, i.e. "Mr. and Mrs. Gerald Thomas." Since handwriting legibility may be a concern, it is helpful to make a numbered list of all your guests and very lightly write corresponding numbers on the back of each response card to double check against your list as the replies start appearing in the mail.

In recent years, it has become common to also include on the response card an area where guests can select their choice of reception entree. While this is a useful tactic for assisting your caterer, it is not considered proper invitation etiquette to request this information on the reply card or within the invitation. Alternatively you may wish to call each guest individually or mail a separate card and self-addressed stamped envelope to convey meal choices once a guest has responded affirmatively if you absolutely need to collect this information prior to your reception.

RESPONSE CARD ENVELOPES A matching envelope is included with the response card. The front of the envelope is printed with the name and address of the person recording the responses, whether this person is the bride, groom, or one of their mothers. The back flap is left blank. Response card envelopes should always have the proper postage already affixed.

timing and tallies

Proper etiquette suggests a long lead-time between when your invitations are mailed and when your wedding occurs. This ensures ample time for your guests to receive your invitations, respond to them, and make their plans accordingly. For weddings where most of the guests are locally based, sending invitations six to eight weeks before the actual date is standard. For weddings where most of the guests will be traveling in from out of town or for destination weddings, a mail date ten to twelve weeks prior to the event should be adequate.

As a general rule, about twenty percent of the people you invite will be unable to attend for various reasons. However, do not allow this information to tempt you to over-invite beyond the capacity of your reception site or budget. It is always surprising to see how many people actually do make the effort to attend, and you cannot recall an invitation once it has been issued unless the wedding has been cancelled or postponed.

sticky etiquette issues

Despite meticulous planning and your best intentions, there are bound to be some awkward situations involving your guests and your wedding invitations. Above all, remain calm and try not to let these situations bother you—keep the focus where it belongs, on your wedding and your marriage. Traditional and modern etiquette offer solutions for navigating these potential minefields.

HERE AND THERE   You'd like to have a small, personal ceremony with a big party afterwards? Fine. You only have room for one hundred at the reception, but can invite whomever you like to the ceremony? Not a good idea. It's really not the same thing. Most people understand if you'd only like a handful present for an intimate ceremony, but limiting your guest list for the fun of the reception might feel exclusionary. If you find yourself in this situation, cut the guest list for the ceremony to match the number you can accommodate at the reception or find a bigger reception space.

THE QUESTION OF KIDS   It is not required that you include children when inviting the parents. It is the personal choice of the bride and groom whether or not to allow children at any part of their wedding. Some couples find children to be a distraction at an otherwise adult celebration, and occasionally there are concerns that a particular reception location may not be a suitable environment for children of a young age. Other couples look upon weddings as a family affair, and are happy to include children in the wedding party and as guests at the reception. Whatever your decision regarding children, be sure to make it applicable across the board to avoid hurt feelings, and resist making any exceptions. And remember, invitations are a call to gather together; under no circumstances should you write "No children, please" or "Adults only" on the invitation. If you address your envelopes properly (to the parents only), your intentions should be understood. To make things crystal clear, you can enlist the aid of your wedding party and family members to help spread the word. Be prepared to accept the fact that some guests may not attend if they have to find a sitter or travel without their kids.

If prior to the wedding you find that parents intend on bringing their uninvited offspring along (either not respecting your wishes as communicated by the invitation or innocently assuming the children are invited), you or the person hosting the event are perfectly within your rights to call and let the parents know that regretfully, no children are invited. Once the wedding is underway, parents who arrive with their brood in tow cannot be turned away, so do your best to graciously accommodate them.

If you do choose to include the little ones, consider any special arrangements their presence may require, such as the need for high chairs or booster seats at the reception. It may also be a good idea to book an adjoining room and hire an on-site babysitter to help look after the kids during the party.

THE "AND GUEST" DEBACLE Unlike the rule governing the inviting of both members of a married or cohabitating couple, it is not mandatory to invite single guests with a date. However as mentioned before, if you are aware that your guest has been seeing someone seriously or if your guest is traveling a long way to be at your wedding and you are able to accomodate some additional people, it is a thoughtful gesture to allow your guest to bring someone along. To be extra gracious, call your guest ahead of time and let him or her know you'd like to extend the invitation to include a date; find out your guest's date's name, and address and send the date his or her own invitation.

Most single guests understand if they are to come alone, but there are three possible unwelcome scenarios that might occur when you don't extend the invitation for your guest to bring a date: your guest may imply via the response card that he or she will be bringing someone, your guest may call and ask if he or she may bring someone, or your guest may show up at your reception with someone. In the first case, you have two choices. You may simply avoid an uncomfortable confrontation with your guest and expand your guest list to accomodate this extra person, or you may call your guest and explain gently but firmly that as much as you would like to allow for everyone to bring someone else along, because of site or budget constraints or the fact that you and your intended wish to have a small, intimate, or close family and friends only wedding, you'll have to ask him or her to attend solo.

Most will understand and appreciate the time you take to call them personally. As for the brazen guest who directly asks about a "plus one" you may politely refuse, for the same reasons above. Unfortunately, those who show up at your wedding accompanied must be calmly accommodated.

WHEN GOOD GUESTS TURN BAD You've made it as easy as possible. You've given a deadline, and you've even stamped the envelope. So why is it so hard for some guests to indicate their reply and pop the response card in the mailbox? Surely their lapse in decorum isn't intentional. But still, you need to know whether or not the person will be coming so you can finalize your headcount and draw up your seating chart. When your deadline has passed and you have not received a response from some of your guests, do not assume they are not coming. Instead, it is perfectly acceptable to take matters into your own hands and call these guests to find out their intentions. Perhaps they thought they did return a response, maybe they misplaced the card, or their response may have been lost in the mail. You, your future spouse, a parent, or members of your wedding party can help make the calls. Whatever the reason, it will put everyone at ease if you and those helping you are gracious, but make no apologies and ask in a simple, direct way. If you cannot reach the guest, make a second call. If you still do not get a response, assume the guest is, in fact, coming as it is better to have food and seating available than not.

Occasionally, last-minute situations such as an unexpected work issue, illness, or travel problem prevent a guest who has responded "yes" from attending. Forgive these guests, and try to make arrangements to see them after the wedding and honeymoon.

UNINVITED GUESTS Sometimes when the phone rings it isn't a guest calling with their good wishes, but someone who isn't invited calling to say, "I haven't received my invitation yet." In these delicate situations, while difficult, it's best to be honest with people. Tell the caller, that unfortunately your number of guests had to be limited because of family constraints, site capacity, your desire for an intimate wedding and that as much as you would have loved to have him or her there it is simply not possible. Most people will understand, and you can follow up the bad news by making a plan to get together when the dust has settled post-honeymoon. After all, the person was kind enough to call and is interested in you and your wedding. One caveat: guests at a engagement party or shower have a right to assume they are to be guests at the wedding, so be sure all these people make the list for the main event.

LEFT OFF THE LIST You, your future spouse, and your parents may all have spent untold hours devising and revising the guest list, to the point where you've looked at it so many times you don't realize you have forgotten to include someone until you have already mailed out the invitations. This is where extra invitations you have ordered will come to your aid. If you are still within the window of six to eight weeks prior to your wedding (even down to four weeks is still acceptable), simply pop another invitation in the mail and the guest will never be the wiser. If you no longer have any invitations you can try to rush a re-order (this may be costly) or you may handwrite or computer-print a replica on pretty paper. Any less than three weeks prior, and your best bet is call the guest. Apologize for not inviting them sooner and let them know how much their presence would mean to you.

ATTENDANCE ANTICIPATION One common quandry that faces many couples is the issue of whether or not to invite people whom they are fairly certain won't attend. First, examine your reasons for inviting these guests in the first place. If you are inviting them because you think they probably won't come (and you'll feel better for having invited them or—worse—hoping they'll send a gift), don't. Only invite those whom you'd really like to have at your wedding, and include them in your headcount because chances are, they just might make the effort to be there. And if they absolutely can't, they'll be happy to have been included.

BOSS AND CO. Although your wedding guest list is undoubtedly dominated by your family and friends there is another group of people you might consider including: your boss and coworkers. After all, you probably spend more time with them than with some of your family members. While you're not required to invite anyone from your office, it is a nice gesture to include your bosses, especially if you have good relationships with them. When it comes to coworkers, invite whom you like, but be sensitive to groups of people—invite quietly and carefully so the non-invited don't feel left out. If you find the number becoming too large, it is probably better not to invite any coworkers at all than to ask a chosen few and risk offending people you have to see every day.

INVITING AN EX Even if you've remained friendly with an ex, it is generally not appropriate for this person to be invited to your wedding. Your wedding is a time to focus on your future with the love of your life, not dredge up old flames. If inviting an ex is somehow unavoidable, for example if the person in question is the son or daughter of family friends who are invited, be sure to discuss the situation with your soon-to-be spouse and make sure you are both comfortable with the arrangements before issuing the invitation.

BRING ON THE "B LIST" Once you've whittled down your guest list to the actual number of people that fit your reception site or budget, you may find yourself with a good number of people whom you'd still love to have present if given the chance. If you send out the first-cut invitations early enough (say, eight weeks prior to the wedding), you may still be able to include guests from the unfortunately named "B list" as any regrets start to come in. This is acceptable, as long as the second round of invitations are mailed at least four weeks before the wedding.

NO QUID PRO QUO An old college friend invited you to her wedding shortly after you graduated. A former colleague put you on the guest list when he tied the knot. You're not really in contact with either of these people anymore, but do you invite them to your wedding anyway since you were there when they got married? In a word, no. There is no need to feel obligated to "pay back" an invitation for an invitation. Your guest list should be comprised only of family and friends you truly wish to witness your marriage. If you want these acquaintances to be there, by all means invite them, but if you simply wish to bring them up to date on your new marital status, feel free to send them a wedding announcement.

THE "GIMME" GAFFE Despite what you hear from your registry source and the special little insert cards they may provide, traditional etiquette says it is in bad form to include details about where you are registered in your wedding invitations because it implies you are expecting a gift. An invitation calls for presence, not presents, so leave it up to your guests to do some sleuthing to find out where you are registered (most will ask your parents or members of the wedding party) if they wish to give you a gift.

ENVISIONING

for many years, an unwavering code of correctness held authority over every aspect of wedding invitations. This code dictated that invitations be rectangular and made of ecru-colored paper with engraved script in black ink. There were absolutely no exceptions. A bride of "good breeding"—or, more likely, her proper and well-meaning parents—wouldn't even dream of being so uncouth as to send wedding guests a square-shaped invitation, let alone one in a bright color or funky font. How times have changed! These days, walk into any stationery store, browse the offerings of an online invitation site, or flip through a catalog and you're likely to be quite surprised (and maybe even a bit overwhelmed) by the sheer volume of possibilities. And while the most formal and classic wedding invitations as described above are still widely available and never go out of fashion, anything goes for modern brides and grooms and you are, of course, free to break from tradition.

page 58 Your invitation may be as simple or elaborate as you wish. Arriving in its own charming box, this invitation is opened like a small gift to reveal an ensemble of coordinating elements.

To find your perfect invitation, start envisioning the look you want about seven to nine months before your wedding. You'll have several style decisions to make, including a choice of printing method, paper type and color, ink color and type font, and the overall size and shape. You may also want to spend some time thinking about a way to make your mark on your invitation with a personal detail, such as a motif, monogram, or photograph. As you take in the breadth of what's available and narrow down your options, keep in mind that all of your selections should work together seamlessly and reflect the general style of your wedding.

printing methods

A good place to begin is with a printing method. There are a number of printing techniques available for use on wedding invitations, and each has its own charms as well as price. Your printing choice may impact your other decisions as well, such as the type of paper you can or should use, or the type-style that might be the most appropriate. Conventional printing methods by stationers and print shops are discussed here. You may choose to print your invitations on your home computer; you'll find information about do-it-your-self options on page 105.

ENGRAVING   The time-honored and most formal means of printing a wedding invitation is still held in high regard for its beauty and classic look. Engraving is easily recognizable by the three-dimensional texture of its slightly raised letters on the front of the invitation as well as a "bruised" appearance on

Mr. and Mrs. Albert Joseph Wakeman

request the honour of your presence

at the marriage of their daughter

Brittany Leigh

to

Dr. Ronald Timothy Duncan

on Saturday, the seventh of July

at half after five o'clock

Saint Luke's Church

Three South Main Street

New York City

the reverse thanks to the intense pressure used when printing. Engraved type has a crisp, saturated color with a matte finish. An engraved invitation exudes elegance as well as expense, for this is the most costly of printing options with a time-consuming process dating back to the nineteenth century. A metal plate (typically copper or steel) is engraved with the type and any images desired in reverse. The plate, or die, is rolled with ink then wiped so the ink only remains in the engraved areas. Next the card or paper is placed face down onto the plate and pressed into the lines of ink, which results in dimensional text on the invitation. While traditional fonts and script styles in black ink are most closely associated with formal engraved invitations, you may use the same engraving process for handwritten type styles or colored inks as well. Engraving works best with papers that are of a substantial weight, such as cardstock. Engraving is available at most major stationers as well as online. Some printers will give or sell you the actual plate used to print your invitations as a keepsake.

THERMOGRAPHY If you love the look of engraving but your budget won't allow it, thermography might be the right printing choice for you. This cost-effective alternative emulates the raised lettering of engraving but has a shiny finish (as opposed to the matte print of engraving) and does not have the telltale bruising on the back. Thermography is created when a resin powder is applied to wet ink, and then heated; the heat causes the powder to swell and fuse to the ink, which results in the textured type or image on the invitation once it dries. Smooth paper works best for this printing technique; textured paper or paper with inclusions such as flower petals should be avoided as the surface might prevent the resin from adhering. Some heavyweight

< The most formal of wedding invitations is engraved. Here, the raised texture
of the engraved type is visible.

papers might not take thermography well, either. Thermography is available at many stationers and through online invitation sites and mail order catalogs.

LETTERPRESS With this printing method, what's old is new again. Letterpress very nearly became a lost art, but has become popular again in recent years. Like engraving, letterpress is an old process — it can be traced to the fifteenth century — and it is also labor-intensive and costly. But that's where the similarities end, as stylistically letterpress is almost the opposite of engraving: The type and any images are debossed on the invitation instead of raised, and raised on the printing plate instead of etched. Letterpress type has a softer, hand-wrought appearance and takes colored ink especially well. The reversed raised type (or image) on the plate is inked and pressure is applied to literally stamp an impression of each letter into the paper. Because of this, a meaty, toothy paper (textured or handmade work well) is essential if you are considering letterpress. This technique is available at many stationers and at independent print shops.

OFFSET LITHOGRAPHY This printing process is known by many names: flat printing, litho, offset litho, offset. Offset printing appears crisp and flat on the paper or cardstock; it is the same type of standard printing you'll find on everyday items like letterhead stationery, ready-made invitations, greeting cards, and fliers. Depending on the overall design of your invitation, offset printing can be informal or formal, or even very modern. The least expensive option generally, it is also the most adaptable. You have your choice of a huge variety of type fonts and ink colors. Many papers may

Letterpress leaves an impression in the paper for a hand-wrought appearance. >
Here, delicate flora and fauna were imprinted first in colored ink,
then the type was printed over the imagery in black ink.

MR. AND MRS. WILLIAM F. PARKER, JR.

AND THE PARENTS OF ERIK BERESFORD

REQUEST THE HONOUR OF YOUR PRESENCE

Dr. and Mrs. Allen Park

request the honour of your presence

at the marriage of their daughter

Rebecca Ann

PRINTING TECHNIQUES FOR DETAILS

Thinking of dressing up your invitations with a special design such as a motif? Consider these additional printing techniques to make your details stand out.

EMBOSSING In this process, an image is imprinted into the paper or card from behind with a die for a raised, relief effect. The embossed area may be inked or left plain (if it is plain it is called blind embossing). Embossing is perfect for a motif, large initial, or a border around an invitation; blind embossing is often used for motifs and monograms as well as the return address on envelope flaps (this is so that the first printed piece that makes an impression for guests is the invitation, not the envelope)

DEBOSSING The opposite of blind embossing; the image is imprinted into the paper or card with a die from the front for an "indented" appearance. Debossing is also good for motifs and monograms.

FOIL STAMPING Also known as foil printing or foil blocking, this process utilizes a die, colored foil, and heat to transfer a shimmering image to an invitation. Many colors are available, and gold and silver are among the most popular. The foil may be matte or shiny. Foil stamping is often used for family crests or singular images without a lot of fine detail.

be printed via offset, but look for those that are very strong and free from additions like petals which may make their surface rough. The offset printing process employs a series of cylinders which transfer the text and any images to the paper. Offset is widely available; some local copy shops might even be able to handle the job, and it's an ideal method for printing invitations you have designed yourself or with the help of a friend. Offset printing is also an interesting choice if you have commissioned a calligrapher to handwrite your invitation; the flat printing style results in every invitation looking like it was actually written by hand.

paper

While it may not seem immediately evident, the paper choice you make for your invitation is not as simple as ivory or ecru. All papers are not created equal. There are handcrafted papers made using centuries-old methods as well as papers produced by machine. Some papers are more suitable for engraving, letterpress or hand calligraphy; at the other end of the spectrum are those made to accommodate modern offset printers and home computer printers. Visually, certain papers present a more formal feeling, while others are designed to express a couple's unique sense of style. Overall, papers vary by content, weight, finish, and color, and each variation contributes something different to the style and quality of your invitation.

CONTENT   At its most basic, paper is matted sheets of fibers. What those fibers are and how the paper is manufactured determines the grade, or quality, of the paper as well as its properties and price. Fine stationery papers are composed by hand or machine of natural cellulose fibers, most commonly one hundred percent cotton, but linen or flax are also used. Often created from leftover rags from the textile industry, they are known as rag papers. These papers resist disintegrating over time, and produce heirloom-worthy keepsake invitations. Some invitation printers produce their own artisanal papers from natural fibers. Second, ranging from medium to high quality, are machine-made papers with a combination of both rag fibers and wood pulp (the percentage of rag fibers is generally noted, e.g. 25% cotton). To imitate the look and feel of handmade papers, good machine-made papers are created using "mold-made" or "pressed finish" techniques and a high percentage of natural fibers. Everyday papers are machine made with a base of cellulose pulp, most commonly from wood but also from straw, reeds, or other materials, both natural and manmade. Some specialty handmade papers may have inclusions of botanical elements such as flower petals, which are lovely for announcing a wedding outdoors or in a garden. If you are having an environmentally friendly "green" wedding, an invitation paper composed of recycled fiber or pulp is a meaningful choice.

WEIGHTS AND WATERMARKS   Paper stock, or the thickness and heaviness of a paper, is judged by how many pounds a ream (500 sheets in a specific size) of the paper weighs. Generally the higher the number, the heavier and thicker the stock—the more expensive the paper. You don't need to know in-depth information about what a paper weighs; simply think of your paper choice in terms of lighter weight (good for folded styles and offset or laser printing), medium weight (a good all-around choice for many styles), or heavy weight (perfect for engraving or letterpress and single panel invitations). The paper stock should compliment the format of your invitation. Some papers may indicate their thickness via ply; for example, a six-ply paper is made of six individual pieces bonded together. The thickness of cardstock, or cover stock, a very stiff and heavyweight paper, is indicated in point sizes, such as 10-pt. card.

Producers of fine papers often mark each piece with a translucent image or logo, known as a watermark, during the papermaking process. In the past, the watermark was used to identify the papermaker and where the paper was made; modern watermarks generally name the paper company and serve as a prestigious sign of quality. The watermark can be viewed from both the front and back of the paper (where it appears in reverse), but the paper should always be printed so the watermark is visible.

FINISH   As you are considering papers, be sure to actually handle a sample and see how it feels for yourself. The surface texture and appearance are collectively known as a paper's finish. Different finishes may affect a paper's printability and receptiveness to ink. Most stationers and printers will be aware of the limitations of a particular paper and only suggest suitable options which complement your choice of printing style, but if you are creating your invitations yourself this is something to be aware of. Note that if you are considering hiring a calligrapher to address your envelopes, certain types of paper are not conducive to the process, such as those with inclusions or coatings. Common paper finishes include:

COATED   An application alters the paper's appearance (e.g. glossy, matte, pearlized)

HANDMADE   Ripples and puckers are made with machines to mimic real handmade paper; also known as cockle finish

LAID   Subtly ridged horizontally and vertically with translucent lines pressed with a special roller into the paper while it's still wet

LINEN   Textured with lines to resemble linen; produced after the paper making process via embossing

PARCHMENT   An antiqued look with a scratchy texture

SMOOTH   The self-explanatory standard; also known as wove finish

VELLUM   Very rich, smooth and creamy

SPECIALTY PAPERS Take a trip to a fine stationer or art supply store to get inspired by the wide range of specialty papers available from all around the world. While some of these papers may be too expensive to be the paper for your actual invitation, they may be used to beautiful effect for the envelope liner, or as an outer wrapping or as an under- or overlay to accent the invitation. In addition to an infinite number of papers printed with patterns by hand or machine, some other special papers you may consider include:

BOTANICAL A paper with natural inclusions such as whole flowers, petals, leaves, or ferns or fronds

CORRUGATED A thick paper or card with pronounced ridges or grooves

GLASSINE A slick, smooth, translucent paper; perfect for overlays or wraps

HANDMADE This term covers a range of papers, which may be crafted of natural materials and plant fibers; the texture may be uneven

INDUSTRIAL Rugged papers including newsprint or those made with recycled papers, as well as cardboard and brown kraft paper

MARBLEIZED A paper embellished with swirls of ink colors to resemble marble

MYLAR Shiny and metallic looking with a mirrored effect

RICE A soft paper, often with inclusions or patterns

VELLUM A translucent paper with a very smooth finish

COLOR SYMBOLISM

Choosing a color for the ink or paper of your wedding invitation can be loaded with meaning. Here are some common positive connotations, however keep in mind that color may represent different—and sometimes opposite—sentiments across cultures.

RED passion, love, celebration, joy, good luck

PINK romance, charm, tenderness

ORANGE energy, vibrance, warmth, change

YELLOW happiness, cheerfulness, peace, courage, hope, faith

BLUE loyalty, fidelity, unity, peace, eternity

GREEN life, nature, fertility, abundance, hope, equality

VIOLET/PURPLE royalty, mystery, spirituality

SILVER richness, purity

GOLD life, light, prosperity, royalty

COLORS For many years, the only acceptable paper color for wedding invitations, according to etiquette, was ivory or ecru (in Europe, the color of choice was always white). These days, if you are having an ultra formal white- or black-tie affair it's probably best to stick with tradition when it comes to paper color. However, if your wedding is less bound by formal custom or you are seeking a creative, contemporary twist, why not experiment with a little color for your invitations? Your invitation's hue might take its cue from your wedding theme, the season, a flower in your bouquet, or your bridesmaids' dresses. It helps to think about a potential ink color in conjunction with your

HOT COLOR DUOS

Thinking of boldly breaking from the ivory/ecru tradition? Consider these chic color combinations for your paper and ink selections.

Chocolate Brown + Pink

Chocolate Brown + Light Blue

Mango + Dark Orange

Grass Green + White

Apricot + Raspberry

Lavender + White

Lavender + Navy

Pale Pink + Hot Pink

Aqua Blue + Red

paper color. While white ink looks lovely on many colored papers, it's more daring to layer color on color, either tonally, such as hot pink ink on pale pink paper, or to use a contrast such as cherry red ink on aqua paper. If you fear going all out with a vivid paper color is a bit too audacious, apply color in moderation on a motif or border, or even as an envelope liner or tissue insert. Or, try a sophisticated mix of neutrals, such as a white or ivory paper with type or accents in beige, taupe, or champagne.

ink

For the most formal and traditional of invitations, black or the somewhat less stark dark gray ink was and still is the way to go. However, contemporary invitations for weddings with a semi-formal or casual bent may experiment creatively with colored inks, either as colored ink on white or ecru paper, colored ink on colored paper, or neutral or white ink on colored paper. If you would like to introduce some colored ink but have reservations about doing your entire invitation this way, you might like to accent black type with a motif or border in a color (keep in mind that printing in more than one ink color increases your printing costs). Metallic inks are also popular, but they work best with engraving. In general, ink colors can vary from printing technique to printing technique, so try to see a printed sample in your chosen ink color and printing style if at all possible. Again, any part of your wedding can provide the inspiration for color. Some printers can custom-blend an ink color to match a specific element of your wedding.

type

Some of the most interesting decisions you'll make for your invitation revolve around how you wish to have the words appear. As with everything, these choices should reflect the look and feel of your wedding as they will send subtle clues to your guests about the formality and style of your affair. And while this is certainly an area to exercise your creativity, remember that the end goal is to fit all of your information on your invitation in an attractive and easily readable way.

PRINTED TYPE STYLES The distinctive appearance of a set of alphabet letters and corresponding characters is known as its typeface, or font. There are literally thousands of typefaces in the world of printing, but for the purposes of most wedding invitations these choices are narrowed down to two general categories, script fonts versus roman and sans serif fonts. Within those two overarching groups you'll still have dozens of options for both traditional and contemporary invitations. Script fonts are slanted and resemble the graceful, fluid swirls of handwritten cursive text; indeed, many of the most popular styles are derived from actual calligraphy hands. Script is generally classic and formal; some versions have very fancy and old-fashioned curlicue accents, but newer forms have also been developed for a cleaner, more modern look that may resemble contemporary handwritting. Roman and sans serif fonts can be formal, very stylized, or informal. Roman fonts have serifs, or decorative lines at the start and finish of each stroke of a letter (such as the type in this sentence), while sans serif fonts do without these decorative lines.

CALLIGRAPHY TYPE STYLES For a truly one-of-a-kind invitation, you may wish to hire a calligrapher to handwrite a single invitation and its accompanying components, which you can then purchase and print via your preferred technique. If you choose to go this route, be sure to allow some extra time in your process for development and review. Beautiful and romantic, the art of calligraphy has its origins in illuminated manuscripts painstakingly hand-lettered by scribes. Traditional calligraphy is handwritten with a pointed pen dipped in ink or a broad-tipped pen. Calligraphy type-

A contemporary invitation might combine different fonts and increase the type size > of the couple's names or meaningful words for added emphasis.

Nancy and Stuart Johnson together
with Elizabeth and Harold Barton
request the honor of your presence at
the marriage celebration of their children

Juliana May Johnson **&** Robert David Barton

on the eleventh day of October
two thousand and three at four o'clock
at Augustus Snow House in Harwichport,
Massachusetts. Reception to follow. **unite**

venetian script — *The honour of your presence*

copperplate script — *The honour of your presence*

spencerian script — *The honour of your presence*

handwriting script — *The honour of your presence*

pointed pen italic — *The honour of your presence*

chancery italic — *The honour of your presence*

celtic — *the honour of your presence*

styles are distinguished by the individual flourishes of each letter, the style of its capital letters and ascending and descending letters, and the pressure used to create thick and thin lines of the letters. Different calligraphers will practice different calligraphy styles, known as hands. There are several popular and widely available hands (see the examples at left). While the written hands resemble the similarly-named printed script versions, keep in mind that each calligrapher will bring his or her own personal nuances to how they scribe a particular hand. Many calligraphers are able to create customized or more elaborate versions of common hands. Some calligraphers might invent their own unique hands, while others may also offer less labor-intensive yet still fanciful handwriting created using a monoline pen instead of a calligraphy nib. These invented or handwriting styles are often excellent choices for penning contemporary invitations.

TYPE TREATMENTS Another decision to make is how the type should lay out on the page. Do you prefer a mix of upper and lower case letters, all capitals, or all lowercase? You'll also need to think about point size, which is the unit of measure for the size of individual letters and characters. For extra emphasis, you can call out the names of the bride and groom or a word or an element like an ampersand in a larger point size than the rest of the wording or even a different—yet complementary—font. Traditional invitations center the type on the paper and stack the information (each line shares a common center point); for a contemporary twist, position all of the text flush left or right, or set it all in the bottom third of the invitation after an expanse of white space. You may experiment with layers of type, such as a semi-sheer printed overlay placed over the main invitation.

COMPOSITION When it comes to the actual physical composition of the invitation, there are more inventive choices than ever before. A couple can choose whatever format appeals (whether flat or folded), any shape to suit their fancy, and a size only constricted by the limits of their postal budget.

FORMAT When thinking about how you want your invitation to look, also think about how much information you need to communicate. This second point may drive the first. Most traditional wedding invitations are either a single panel or a bi-fold, but weddings with a need to convey a lot of information or packed with multiple enclosures may best be served by roomy tri-fold or accordion styles. Basic formats include:

accordion A long piece of paper or card stock is folded back and forth to create a multi-paneled invitation; the front and back panels serve as covers.

bi-fold Medium-weight paper folded to open like a book; the invitation copy may be printed on the outside front cover with the interior left blank, or a monogram or motif can appear on the cover with the invitation text printed on the inside.

french fold A sheet of paper is folded twice to create a four-paneled invitation; the invitation copy may be printed on the cover or inside as in the bi-fold style; most often done with lighter weight papers.

scroll Generally done with lightweight paper, a long sheet is printed with all the invitation text and rolled; requires a tube for mailing.

short-fold A piece of paper or card is folded, not exactly in half, to create a short front panel and longer back panel.

An outer envelope is unnecessary with this foldout style invitation; the main message, >
covered with a decorative sheet of vellum, is framed by the flaps when it's opened.

single panel Also known as a flat card; an invitation of one single piece with type printed on one side; most luxurious in heavyweight cardstock; may have a sheer overlay.

tri-fold Also known as a C-fold; card or paper is folded from two opposite edges (either horizontally or vertically) to produce three panels; the two outer panels are folded inward (either overlapping or with their edges meeting) to cover the center panel. The folds may be decorative or provide a place to insert enclosures such as a reply card, itinerary, or accommodations information.

z-fold Paper is folded twice in accordion fashion to form a three-paneled invitation.

SHAPE AND SIZE Traditional formal invitations are a vertical rectangle in a single panel or bi-fold format. The rectangle even has standardized sizing: 4^{1}/2 x 6^{1}/4 inches and 5^{1}/2 x 7^{1}/2 inches, known as classic and embassy sizes, respectively. In recent years the square, or marquise, style has increased in popularity as well as the tea length style, which is a narrow, elongated rectangle, sometimes with a semi-sheer overlay. You can choose squared or rounded corners for any of these shapes. You may also encounter circular or oval options, but these can be more expensive than more common rectangle and square shapes. Keep in mind that large or unusually shaped invitations will often require additional postage.

embellishments

In the same way you accent your wedding gown with accessories and trimmings such as lace or beading, you may wish to dress up your wedding

SEASONAL SYMBOLS

Let the time of year of your wedding guide your symbol selection—every season is rife with inspiration.

SPRING	FALL
Basket of Flowers	Acorn
Chick	Apple
Spring Leaf	Autumn leaf
Tulip	Cornucopia
Tree	Sunflower

SUMMER	WINTER
Beach Ball	Holly
Bee	Pair of Mittens
Dragonfly	Pine Bough or Cone
Shell	Snowflake
Sun	Wreath

invitation with embellishing elements. Motifs, linings, decorative extras, and charming details all lend a truly personalized touch to an invitation.

MOTIFS One of the easiest ways to decorate your invitation is with a motif; this signature symbol can become your logo and visually unify all of the pieces of your wedding stationery, including your save-the-date cards, programs, reception stationary, favors and thank you cards. Many stationers offer ready-made motifs, however you may commission a graphic artist to make a special design for you. You might even download clip art off the internet or find an interesting image in an old book (just be sure not to infringe on any copyright laws). For inspiration, think about something that

MOTIFS & MEANINGS

Give your invitation some matrimonial meaning with one of these classic motifs. Not surprisingly, there are many representing marriage-minded themes of fidelity and fertility.

ACORN = life, beginnings

ANCHOR = hope, stability

ANKH = Egyptian symbol for life and immortality

APPLE = fertility, love

BAMBOO = lasting friendship, devotion

BEE = faithfulness

BIRD = the soul

BRIDGE = transition from one life to another

BUTTERFLY = the soul, joy

CHRYSANTHEMUM = happiness, longevity

CLASPED HANDS = union, friendship

CORNUCOPIA = abundance

COWRIE SHELL = fertility

DAISY = innocence, purity

DICE = fate

DOG = fidelity

DOUBLE HAPPINESS = Chinese symbol for joy

DOVE = life spirit, soul

ELEPHANT = fidelity, conjugal felicity

EVERGREENS = eternity

FEATHER = truth

FERN = sincerity

FISH = a pair portrays the joys of union and marriage

FLEUR-DE-LYS = hope, affection

FROG = fertility, harmony between lovers

GATE = entrance into new life

HOLLY = good will, joy

HORSESHOE = good luck

IVY = constant affection, friendship, fidelity

KNOT = union

LADYBUG = luck

LOTUS = past, present, and future; love

LUTE = connubial bliss, friendship

MAPLE LEAF = emblem of lovers

PALM TREE = blessings

PEACOCK = love, desire

PEONY = love, good fortune, happiness

PINEAPPLE = fertility, hospitality

PINE CONE = good fortune

POMEGRANATE = fertility, posterity

ROSE = passion, desire, joy

SHELL = life, love, marriage, good fortune

STARFISH = divine love

SUNFLOWER = infatuation, longevity

TREE = the life principle, diversity in unity

TULIP = perfect love

WREATH = a happy fate, good luck, fertility, marriage

YIN YANG = complementary opposites, balance of two forces represents the two of you as a couple or something that is unique to your wedding in particular. The season, location, or theme of your wedding may inspire your motif selection, as would any image that means something special to you (say a lamppost if you got engaged underneath one) or signifies an interest you share (such as a violin for a pair of classical musicians). One variation is to choose a main motif for your invitation (such as a tree) and diffuse the imagery over the course of the enclosures (i.e. putting leaves from the tree on the reception card, response card, etc.) Or, consider a simple nuptial emblem such as a dove or pair of interlocking rings. If your family has a crest or coat of arms, a formal invitation is the perfect place to display it. You can't get any more personal than a monogram—single first-name initials (J & A) or two sets of initials (J.C. & A.T.), are the best options, as a monogram with a main last name initial surrounded by your two first name initials wouldn't be technically correct on your invitation as you aren't yet married and don't yet share the same last name. A motif may be printed using the same process and ink color as the type on your invitation, or you may choose to have it stand out with a technique like embossing or foil stamping or even a second ink color. For a less detailed motif, a die-cut silhouette could be a lovely alternative to printing.

BORDERS Understated and classic, a border is a simple decoration that provides complementary texture or color to your invitation design while keeping the focus on the words. A border may be printed or embossed, with or without an ink color. An embossed thick or thin rule line or panel framing the copy is the most classic, but dozens of more intricate designs such as colored lines, beading, scrolls, or vines are also possibilities.

EDGE TREATMENTS Another subtle decorative option is to embellish the edges of the invitation. Deckled edges are irregular and unfinished with a torn appearance; handmade paper is naturally deckled, but other papers may reproduce this antique and handcrafted effect artificially. Edges can also be beveled for an elegant three-dimensional look, cut with a pattern such as scalloping, or colored with ink to match the printing or lining of the invitation.

TISSUES, OVERLAYS, WRAPS, AND LINERS Beyond the material of the main invitation, additional papers add intrigue to the overall design. If you have ordered engraved invitations, they may be delivered to you with tissue separating each piece. In years past, these tissues served a definite purpose: ink was slow to dry, and the tissue was laid on top of the printing to prevent smudging. Modern printing inks no longer have smudging as an issue, so the inserted tissue is merely decorative and you may choose to include it or discard it as you see fit. For a twist on this tradition, you might wish to insert a tissue in a complementary color rather than the standard ivory or white. Overlays in translucent papers such as vellum or glassine produce a muting effect to what lies underneath; alternatively, the overlay may be printed with a pattern, image, or text and held in place over the invitation via ribbon, grommets, glue, or another secure means. Sometimes, the words to the invitation itself are printed on the overlay. Translucent wraps around the invitation work in a similar fashion, or you can use a wrap in

< Choose a motif that resonates with the two of you as a couple. A tree may recall the oak under which you became engaged, the strength of your love, or the spring season in which you will be wed.

patterned or textured paper to introduce some visual interest. A liner underneath the envelope flap in a contrasting color or pattern is a pretty decorative
touch. Some etiquette rules to note: For a single outer envelope, a liner is not
required; however, a liner should be used with an inner envelope (in this
case, subsequently lining the outer envelope is optional).

VISUAL IMAGERY If mere words aren't enough for you to convey your
joy about your impending nuptials, you might like to say it in pictures.
Printing your invitation with a photograph of the two of you together as you
are now or individually as children can be personal and charming. For less
formal weddings, you could substitute a whimsical line drawing of you both.
A photograph of your wedding location lightly printed as a background for the
invitation copy would give your guests something to look forward to—this is
an especially enticing idea for a destination wedding. For a one-of-a-kind look
for smaller weddings, you might commission a calligrapher or artist to inscribe
each invitation with a hand-colored illustration or botanical drawing.

FASTENERS Invitations with a couple of pages or multiple enclosures
may need some means of keeping everything together or they risk looking
unkempt. Classic or more formal invitations can remain organized with the
help of a tri-fold format with pockets or tied lengths of cording or ribbon or
a paper belly band wrapped around the bundle. Contemporary invitations
might make use of industrial grommets, chic paper clips, raffia, or ingenious
stitching with needle and thread to hold pieces in their place. Stitching is

A photograph may be incorporated into your design to glorious effect, either as a >
wrap around the rest of your invitation or as an overlay over the text.

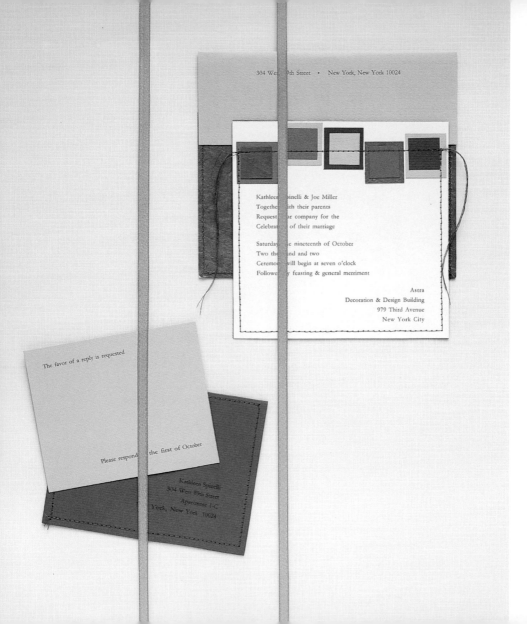

304 West 90th Street • New York, New York 10024

Kathleen Spinelli & Joe Miller
Together with their parents
Request your company for the
Celebration of their marriage

Saturday the nineteenth of October
Two thousand and two
Ceremony will begin at seven o'clock
Followed by feasting & general merriment

Astra
Decoration & Design Building
979 Third Avenue
New York City

The favor of a reply is requested

Please respond by the first of October

Kathleen Spinelli
304 West 89th Street
Apartment 1-C
New York, New York 10024

also an interesting way to bind individual panels together for bi-fold or tri-fold invitations or adhere a sheer overlay of paper or fabric to an invitation.

LITTLE EXTRAS There are those brides who believe that embellishment is everything when it comes to their wedding. If you count yourself among their number, feel free to decorate your invitation with any of these lovely little extras as you see fit. Bows, metal charms, and appliqued pressed flowers or leaves add a feminine flair to an invitation (however, if the groom is the type who might balk at the sight of such girliness, forgo these details for the sake of pre-matrimonial harmony). For a gesture hearkening back to Renaissance times, finish off the flap of each envelope with a wax seal. Or, if your budget allows, send each guest a boxed keepsake invitation presented like a small gift—for example, a message in a bottle filled with sand, shells, and your invitation for a beach wedding or a tiny bottle of maple syrup attached to your invitation for a wedding in Vermont.

A FEW WORDS If you've got something you'd like to say, your wedding invitation offers a very personal platform upon which to say it. A few tasteful words—borrowed from a favorite author, poet, psalmist, composer, or sonneteer—offer guests a window into your intertwined souls. Some contemporary-style invitations might even tell a short story—your story, that is, of your engagement or first date—leading up to the details of the big day.

⟨ Artful embellishments, such as these sewn squares, enhance semi-formal invitations. The color palette carries through to each piece in the ensemble to make a cohesive statement.

IT IS WITH JOY THAT WE,

Vicky Galinato Mara,
and
Timothy Kevin Story

INVITE YOU TO SHARE IN OUR CELEBRATION OF LOVE
AS WE EXCHANGE MARRIAGE VOWS
AND BEGIN OUR NEW LIFE TOGETHER
SATURDAY, THE TWENTY THIRD OF AUGUST
TWO THOUSAND AND THREE
AT FOUR O'CLOCK IN THE AFTERNOON

CREATING

having familiarized yourself with printing methods and paper choices, and having survived the ins and outs of etiquette and wording, it's at last time to bring your invitations to life. But once you know what you want, how do you get what you need? There are several ways to create wedding invitations, either with the help of professionals or by your own hand. Each approach has its own pros and cons, not the least of which is cost and timing. If you choose to work with professionals such as a stationer, printer, or calligrapher, you'll generally need to book a preliminary appointment to discuss their services and review their offerings. If you'll be purchasing your invitations via catalog or online, or producing them yourself, you of course can do so on your own time. In any event, before you move forward down any of these roads be sure to review your roster of critical information—your wedding style, total number of invitations needed (remember this is generally not the same as the

page 90 You can incorporate fancy, decorative elements such as ribbon or fabric for a striking effect.

actual number of people on your guest list), anticipated enclosure needs, time constraints, and budget—once more so you can make informed decisions during this creative process. You'll need to establish which means you're going to use to create your invitations about six or seven months prior to your wedding as you'll need to place the order or start to create them yourself between three and five months before the wedding. You want to leave yourself plenty of time to complete the process without rushing and get the invitations in the mail on time. For the following, keep in mind that individual paper professionals will have established their own processes and timing.

working with a stationer

Stationery stores are a popular destination for many brides-to-be. Not only do they stock a selection of custom order invitations, printable invitations, and do-it-yourself invitation supplies and papers, but they also usually offer a range of other wedding paper needs including thank you notes, favor supplies, guest books, and photo albums. Most stationers act as dealers, carrying different invitation lines while sometimes offering their own custom versions. Samples from various invitation companies as well as each company's individual ordering policies are usually organized in binders which you can flip through in the store to get a sense of options and the price ranges. If you don't find what you're looking for in the stationer's selection of wedding invitations, don't overlook the rest of their resources; you might discover something totally appropriate for your wedding in their samples for custom-printed invitations for regular parties. Know too that some high-end stationers might also be able to assist you in the creation of one-of-a-kind invitations you make yourself, or might even host special wedding workshops on the premises.

While many stationers do not mind walk-ins for binder browsing, it is often best to book an appointment with an invitation consultant on staff who can help guide you to just the right examples of what you may be looking for or who can advise you on what type of invitation might be the best choice for your wedding. The consultant should be able to offer tips on etiquette, printing methods, and style and answer any questions you may have. This may take more than one appointment. Note that you will probably have a consultant's full attention if you schedule an appointment on a weekday instead of a busy weekend. Once you decide on a particular style (including paper, type, ink color, and printing method) you'll discuss and finalize wording with the consultant then place the order for your invitation and any accompanying enclosures. You will also review the overall process and timing, sign off on an order form or contract, and pay a deposit (most require fifty percent).

FINDING A STATIONER Local stationers are easily accessible, and chances are you may have friends who have used their services and can tell you about their experiences. If no stationers immediately come to mind, browse the yellow pages or use internet search engines to scope out some potential options in your area. Larger chain stationers as well as smaller independent stationers almost always stock wedding invitations. You can investigate the designs of many invitation companies online (see the Resources section on page 151); most sites will refer you to stationers in your area who carry their products. The benefits of working with a stationer include one-on-one service, the security that they've done it before, their connections with top-of-the-line printers, and their assortment of brand name papers, and relatively competitive prices. You are limited, of course, to choosing from the lines your particular stationer offers.

STATIONER PRICING Many high-end invitation companies sold by stationers will price their invitations by each individual piece which you may order in set quantities (i.e. 50 pieces, 100 pieces, 125 pieces, etc.); other companies will offer a set price for an entire invitation ensemble consisting of the invitation, outer envelope, inner envelope, reception card, reply card, and reply envelope. Since stationers are essentially middlemen, you are paying a markup price as opposed to going directly to the actual invitation source. For the most part, this is unavoidable as the majority of invitation companies only offer their products through stationers instead of dealing with consumers directly. The stationer's costs may vary based on the brands offered and whether there is competition in the area from other stationers, so it might help to shop around and compare prices for invitations that interest you. Depending on the type of invitation you choose, pricing can range widely from just a couple of dollars an invitation to thirty dollars and higher for specialized models.

working with a designer or printer

Not content with the same offerings available to everyone at your local stationer? You may wish to commission an independent designer or printer to create a custom invitation for you. Think of this option as the ultimate collaboration to make something truly representative of your personal style as a couple. With custom work, the world is your oyster—your choices for papers, inks, embellishments, artwork, or high-quality printing techniques are endless. You can collaborate on an invitation that is truly one-of-a-kind, perhaps incorporating a family photo or a custom monogram. And, accordingly, this type of invitation can take a considerable amount of time and multiple appointments to produce as there is no precedent to follow. Though the methods may vary depending on the individual, you typically would have an initial meeting with the designer or printer to discuss the general details and stylistic needs of your wedding, perhaps the season, theme, or color scheme. You'll be asked—and will have the opportunity to ask—a lot of questions about the type of invitation you desire. After you meet, the designer or printer would then spend some time developing concepts. At another meeting you would review concepts or mockups of potential invitations and offer feedback before finalizing the design and wording and getting a price quote. If the back-and-forth of the creative process doesn't appeal to you, but you're still looking for something beyond the ordinary, you can inquire if the designer or printer has a selection of exclusive or limited-edition original designs you can choose from to reproduce with your own wedding information.

FINDING A DESIGNER OR PRINTER While smaller design and printing operations are somewhat more difficult to find, it is certainly possible. You may get referrals from friends who have taken the independent route, or search online for designers or small print shops in your area. Art schools or art supply stores may also be able to direct you toward some potential connections. Once you locate a few, you may wish to pay a cursory visit to their studios prior to making a working appointment to examine examples of their previous work to see if the designer or printer's style is simpatico with what you have in mind. Or, enquire whether the designer or printer has a website; you may be able to get a sense of his or her style from your own home. If you don't know anyone who has worked directly with your designer or printer before, it is a good idea to ask for contact information for previous clients for reference. When you call, ask the previous clients if they were happy with the work and if they received it on time (critical), if they were able to communicate well with the designer or printer (you want someone you can work with easily), and whether or not they felt like the printer or designer understood what they were looking for (you want to know the person will "get" what you're after without a lot of unnecessary revisions).

CUSTOM INVITATION PRICING With custom work, it's hard to put a finger on exact costs as they can vary widely and depend on the individual choices you make with regards to things like paper and printing technique as well as the experience and demand of the particular designer or printer. However generally speaking, custom invitations are comparatively expensive to readily available styles as you are working directly with the professional for their time and service. Although quotes might not be given until a design is near finalized, you can ask a designer or printer to ballpark what your job might cost to give you a basic idea of whether or not this method will work within your budget. You should understand what all the costs are for your different variables: materials, labor, design, quantity.

working with a calligrapher

Although often associated with addressing envelopes, calligraphy is another means of creating an exclusive invitation unique to your particular wedding. With a handcrafted personality and character that is different from a type font, invitations done by a calligrapher can be both traditional and unique. You can hire a calligrapher to exquisitely handwrite a single copy of your invitation, which can then be printed in quantity using whichever method you wish. The calligrapher can either handle the paper buying and printing for you, or he or she may simply sell you the camera-ready artwork or create a digital file and you can source paper and printers yourself. You would meet with the calligrapher as you would an independent designer or printer to discuss the potential look and feel of your invitation.

When you choose calligraphy for your invitations, the words take the starring role. Many calligraphers recommend that the calligraphy be the main design of the invitation and not compete with preprinted backgrounds, embossing, or other designs. An invitation written in a swirling, traditional hand and printed via engraving is a classic, while a more casual hand printed via letterpress offers another feeling entirely. Couples should be cognizant of how many lines of text they want on their invitation, as it is difficult to include a large amount of writing when lettering by hand.

Before you start to search for a calligrapher, you'll want to get an idea of the style of calligraphy you like. Flip through some calligraphy books to

In addition to scribing the wording, a calligrapher may >
have the talent to create a hand-drawn border or other accents
like these daisies for a one-of-a-kind invitation.

26 Ravenswood Terrace
Cheektowaga, New York
14225

Stephanie Gamble
and
Kevin Colosimo
together with their parents
Thomas and Linda Gamble
Frank and Camille Colosimo
ite you to join in the celebration
of their marriage
aturday, the second of November
Two thousand and two
t one o'clock in the afternoon
Saint Peter's Catholic Church
Wellsboro, Pennsylvania

view different styles or see the guide on page 76. Not every calligrapher scribes every style, so you'll want to look for a professional who already practices the style you are seeking. To find a calligrapher, you may again ask friends, search the web, or inquire at an art school that offers calligraphy classes. There are also good professional calligraphy organizations and guilds with member listings you can peruse (see page 155 in the Resources section). Thanks to the internet and email, it is not necessary to book someone locally.

Keep in mind that there are many variations in calligraphic skill. There is the hobbyist calligrapher who may practice infrequently and the trained artist who has spent years honing his or her craft. Once you have some prospects in mind, you'll want to ask them a few questions to assess their level of experience and see if they can scribe the style you like. Questions like "How long have you been practicing calligraphy professionally?", "How did you learn your technique?", "How many invitations do you create per year?", and "Which hands do you offer?" are a good jumping off point for this discussion. Next you'll need to review some examples of the calligrapher's work. Some calligraphers will have a website with examples, others will have samples or a style sheet to fax, email, or show you in person, while others will mail you actual samples (hopefully in an envelope penned by hand so you can see his or her addressing skills, too). Seeing the actual samples is the most helpful, even if you have to pay a small fee for the calligrapher to send them to you. Request more than one style of calligraphy to get a feel for the calligrapher's range. As you look at the portfolio of the calligrapher's work or samples, pay attention to the rhythmic flow and relative consistency of the letters, the straightness and spacing of the words and lines, and the overall layout, all of which should be balanced and pleasing to the eye. Of course you can and should request contact information for client references from previous projects (ask similar questions to those listed for references for independent designers or printers; see page 97).

CALLIGRAPHER PRICING Custom designed calligraphy for invitations can be expensive as it involves several extra steps beyond invitations offered by a stationer or even custom designed typeface invitations. Furthermore, the difference in individual calligrapher's prices can be vast. Some charge by the piece (invitation, reply card, etc.), some by the line, and still others for an entire invitation ensemble. Be sure you understand what your chosen calligrapher's stance is with regards to fees and pricing. You might be able to set up some sort of package rate if you commission the calligrapher to scribe other items like envelopes, seating cards, and place cards in addition to your invitation template. If you adore the look of calligraphy, but find the cost prohibitive to have your complete invitation created this way, you can elect to have your two names or a monogram written by hand and added to a typeset invitation as artwork.

shopping online or by mail-order

If you enjoy shopping from home, or if you're a bride who's short on time or has a job that doesn't allow for a lot of outside appointments, a website or mail-order catalog can be a good source for invitations.

ONLINE Companies on the web can offer a huge selection of invitations and day or night shopping convenience. A few interesting sites are listed in the Resources section starting on page 155, but you'll also find links to online stationers from most wedding web sites and through internet search

POINTS FOR THE CONTRACT

Before you place an order for invitations, make sure you have all the details down in writing so you and your stationer, calligrapher, or invitation company are all on the same page, so to speak, and understand your obligations to one another. An invitation contract should include information with regards to:

- Bride and groom's names and contact info
- Name of sales person
- Outline of services to be performed (i.e. invitation printing, envelope stuffing)
- Quantities of individual elements (i.e. 150 engraved invitations, 150 reply cards, 175 outer envelopes) or ensembles and what is included (i.e. 150 invitation ensembles including invitation, reception card, reply card and envelope, inner envelope, outer envelope, plus 35 each extra inner and outer envelopes)
- Printing method (engraving, letterpress, offset, etc.)
- Design details for font/typestyle, ink color, paper color, paper size
- Brand of paper and envelopes
- Itemized rates
- Any additional charges (such as those for extra ink colors or additions like ribbon or overlays)
- Specifics regarding customer supplied artwork
- Cancellation policies and fees
- Mistake/redo policies and fees
- Disclaimers (such as variations in handmade papers is to be expected)
- Proof information (expected date, any applicable charges for changes, etc.)
- Project completion date
- Delivery date, means, fees, and address
- Method of payment
- Sales tax, if applicable
- Total charges
- Deposit amount submitted; remainder amount and due date

engines, as well as in advertisements in bridal magazines. Some of the sites are partner to traditional bricks-and-mortar establishments or print catalogs. Most sites are well organized so you can shop easily by theme, color scheme, or shape. The best online sites have useful interactive tools and features you won't find in a paper catalog: for example, you may have the ability to type in your information (bride's name, groom's name, wedding date, etc.) and see an instant mock up of your invitation wording in the style you're considering. You may also be able to experiment with a variety of fonts and color-ways to view the same invitation with different options, and type in your quantities needed for specific items to get instant price quotes. Some sites allow you to "send to a friend"; you can earmark a few designs and forward them to your groom, mom, or maid of honor to show them what you're thinking. Online companies may carry a full assortment of brand-name invitations or they may only have their exclusive designs; samples should be available for purchase. Etiquette tips and wording examples are generally offered, but make sure there is a toll-free number you can call should you run into any problems or have any questions about your order. Some sites will also stock coordinating companion pieces such as seating cards or thank you notes. And as with their sister invitation catalogs, online companies offer fairly quick turnarounds for the finished product. However since the onus is on you to enter your information correctly and your order will be printed exactly as you entered the information, the proofing process is particularly important (again have at least two people proofread your order before you actually submit it). One obvious last note: be sure you are ordering from a secure site if you will be entering your credit card number to place an order.

MAIL ORDER CATALOGS   As soon as you indentify yourself as a bride-to-be and write down your name and address and wedding date for just about anything—logging on to a wedding web site, signing up for a bridal event at a department store, starting a registry, etc.—you might find yourself bombarded (unless you specifically request not to be) with marketing mail for honeymoon destinations, bachelorette party locations, bridal party gift ideas, and the like. One upshot is that you will probably also automatically receive invitation mail-order catalogs. Alternatively, you may see an ad for an invitation catalog in a bridal magazine and call a toll-free number to order a copy, or search the internet to find catalog/online e-tailer combinations.

Invitation catalogs offer convenience and very competitive pricing. Some catalogs may even offer promotions where invitations are less than a dollar each. Mail order catalogs also score high points for quick turnover; some companies offer your completed invitations within just a couple days of placing your order. These catalogs are usually produced directly by the invitation printing company, and the great thing about them, like any catalog, is that you can browse them at your leisure wherever you are— waiting for a gown fitting, on the bus on your way to work, in your bed in your pajamas. Designed to appeal to the widest audience, invitation catalogs often show a very wide range of styles from classic to whimsical to themed, so there is usually something for everyone. Catalog photographs often show an entire invitation ensemble, so you can see how the corresponding reply cards, envelope flaps, and other elements like place cards will all look together.

If you find an invitation you like, you just call or fax in your order. You are responsible for carefully filling in all your wording information correctly on the order form (have at least two people read your order form for possible errors); many catalogs provide wording and etiquette reference, and offer a number to call if you have specific questions or need some guidance. However, what you gain in convenience from shopping from a catalog you may lose in creative leeway as generally you have to buy the invitations as they are with not a lot of room to tinker with their design, paper, fonts, and other details. And of course, you cannot immediately see and feel any samples that interest you; most catalogs offer to sell you actual physical samples for a nominal fee which usually can be applied to your eventual order. Offset printing and thermography are most commonly the printing style available in invitation catalogs, but you will also find some that offer engraving.

doing it yourself

For hands-on brides looking to immerse themselves into every creative detail of their wedding or those to-be-weds in a financial crunch hoping to save some money, DIY invitations might be a fitting solution. Within the concept of DIY there are varying levels of participation, from simply running ready-made invites through your home computer printer to actually designing your own invitation from scratch and taking it to a professional printer for output to taking a class that will give you the skills to execute a particular method on your own. Whichever tack you take, be realistic in your capabilities and make sure you have ample time to get the job done. Creating your invitations yourself should be an enjoyable task, not a laborious one, and the last thing you want to do is ratchet up your stress level before the big day.

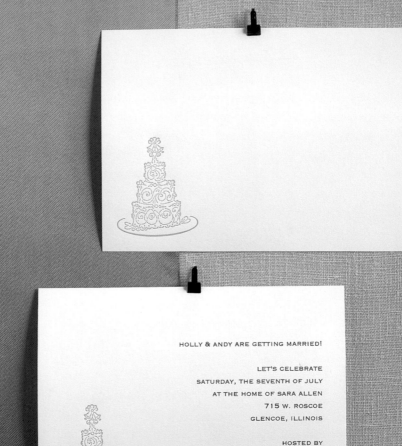

HOLLY & ANDY ARE GETTING MARRIED!

LET'S CELEBRATE
SATURDAY, THE SEVENTH OF JULY
AT THE HOME OF SARA ALLEN
715 W. ROSCOE
GLENCOE, ILLINOIS

HOSTED BY
SARA, KATHY, MOLLY & JANE

RSVP TO JANE 847-243-7482

NO GIFTS PLEASE

PRINTING WITH IMPRINTABLES Perhaps the most foolproof and timely way to tackle creating your invitations yourself is to purchase a set of ready-made stationery known as imprintables, which are designed to run through your standard laser printer. These invitations may have a simple border or they may have a preprinted image with blank space to accommodate your choice of invitation wording. Many adorable wedding designs are out on the market at stationery stores and paper supply stores, but non-wedding themes could also be suitable for casual weddings. All you would need to do is type your information into a simple word processing program on your computer and set it up to print within the appropriate area on the card (it may take a few trial runs to get the correct positioning if you are not accustomed to desktop publishing). Alternatively, you could type up the information and take the imprintables to your local print shop for a more professional-looking printing; overall, this process would still generally run less than ordering invitations traditionally.

USING COMPUTER SOFTWARE A step up from imprintables in terms of your level of responsibility is to create and print your invitations yourself on your own computer with the help of wedding invitation software. Some software will come with paper for you to use, others will need you to select your own papers. Invitation software is available at stationery stores and online, and most programs offer step by step instructions to walk you through the process. Some even include all the paper and materials you will need as

< Imprintables allow you to print invitations on your home computer or you may take them to a printer instead. Choose an imprintable of fine paper or one that features something special like this letterpress-printed cake for a professional look.

a kit. You may have a few design options to choose from, and some software some might even have additional features such as bonus programs for "new house" or "new baby" stationery (nothing like thinking ahead) or a built-in address book to store your guest list details. Each software package is different, but most ask you to input your information into a template, which will create your invitation using a common format and wording. You then just print out your invitations via your home printer.

DESIGNING YOUR OWN INVITATIONS   For the most personal invitations, true individualists with the time and the skills can consider designing wedding invitations themselves, either on their own or with the help of a graphic designer friend. Your own design can be very unique, perhaps with a special wedding logo you've created or incorporating photos of the two of you or family wedding photos through the years. You can elect to print the invitations on your home printer if it is of a good quality, or prepare the file to be printed professionally on fine paper or cardstock via offset, letterpress, or engraving. Professional printers base their rates on quantity, so if you have a small guest list it might be wise to print the invitations yourself. Desktop publishing applications such as QuarkXpress, Illustrator, or InDesign are acceptable by most printers.

Here are the general steps you might take to create your own invitations:

PARTNER WITH A PRINTER   Partner with a service bureau, a reputable printing business accustomed to printing commercial items as well as personal projects. Your printer will be able to give you some preliminary advice as well as guidelines and tips along the way. Be sure to enquire about

PRE-PRINT PROOFING

Whether you work with a professional or set up your own virtual print shop in your home, it pays to proof your invitation before going to press. And though your stationer, mail order catalog, calligrapher, or online invitation company might charge you a fee to arrange for a proof, it is a small price to pay for peace of mind and an invitation that is 100% accurate. Generally, you would receive a black and white proof via fax or email (some printers might occasionally offer a full color proof). You would read the proof carefully, and get at least one other pair of eyes to read it with you to check and double check for spelling, mistakes, typos, and errors in pertinent information which might be easy to miss. If any errors are, in fact, present, by all means speak up as this is the time to correct them. Mark up the proof with pencil or document all your requests for changes in writing. If you make corrections, a second proof should be reviewed. When everything is correct, at last your invitation goes to press.

specifications they may require, and make sure they accept files in the same application (QuarkXpress, Illustrator, etc), platform (Mac or PC), and version in which you are working.

CHOOSE YOUR PAPERS AND ENVELOPES Be sure to select a paper compatible with the type of printing process you plan on using.

ESTABLISH YOUR FORMAT Generally, it's easiest and most cost-effective to stick with standard sizes. Remember that the envelopes should be the right size for the job. If you create a custom-sized invitation, getting custom envelopes made could be costly. Remember that one-sided printing will always be less expensive than two, as will one-color printing.

PREPARING A FILE FOR A PRINTER

DO talk with your service bureau or printer to clarify what they need from you to make the job go smoothly. Ask lots of questions—their job is to answer any of your production questions and provide you with a finished product that meets your needs.

DO think everything through before you go to press and sign off on final proofs (Do my invites fit inside the envelope I have chosen? Are all of my colors consistent? Are my graphics in the right format?)

DO be as thorough with your instructions and organization of your files as possible. Include all fonts, graphics and layouts in an organized folder system.

DON'T rush through the proofing stage. You may miss a typo or an error and be stuck with a finished printed product that is not what you want. It is your job to catch typos and errors in your document, not the job of your service bureau.

DON'T experiment with design techniques you may not have a lot of experience using (i.e. designing your invitation with light inks on dark papers)

DON'T be afraid to ask questions of your service bureau.

DESIGN YOUR FILE Create any motifs, choose any artwork or photos, decide how many colors you will use (this affects printing costs), and write your text. Use crop marks to indicate trim (actual) size of your finished document. If you plan on using a photograph in your design, check with your service bureau to determine how high the resolution should be and what format they require (e.g. EPS, TIFF), and include an extra uncompressed copy of the image when submitting your file.

DO YOUR PRE-PRESS TASKS Gather all necessary components (document layout, fonts, graphics) for your file.

DO YOUR PRE-FLIGHT TASKS Double-check your pre-press work, if possible with an onscreen preview of all the elements of your invitation.

DELIVER YOUR FILE TO YOUR SERVICE BUREAU Be sure to enquire what types of delivery formats they accept (Zip disc, CD, electronic submission via FTP or email). Label any discs with your name and phone number. It is also advised to include this information as a "Read Me" file on your disc. Make a backup file and retain it in case anything goes wrong. Make sure you are clear about all instructions for printing (printing process, selected paper/envelope types, etc.), and include a laser-printed version of how you expect your document to appear (that way, the service bureau can easily see if there are any problems with the file they have as compared to your laser printout). Always include the fonts that you have used in your document; if your service bureau doesn't have a font that you have used in your document and you provide the font file (found in your computer's system folder), they can install the font. Include the entire font suitcase for a font so that all versions (italic, bold, etc.) of the font are included, as well as all formats (screen and printer versions of the font).

APPROVE YOUR PROOF FROM YOUR SERVICE BUREAU

RECEIVE YOUR FINAL PRINTED PRODUCT

QUANTIFYING QUANTITIES

Keep these important tips in mind when calculating your invitation numbers.

ACTUAL INVITES This number does not equal the number of guests on your guest list; remember couples share an invitation as do families with children unless they are over 18.

EXTRA INVITES Plan on inviting a B-list? Need to hand out a lot of keepsakes? Suspect your guest list might expand? Be sure to order enough extras (at least 25) as reprinting your invites at a later date can be costly.

EXTRA ENVELOPES Addressing mistakes can happen, either by your own hand or that of your calligrapher. Tack on an extra 15-20% more envelopes than you actually need to take this into consideration.

TAKING A CLASS Doing your invitations yourself is an opportunity to broaden your artistic horizons. If you are so inclined and also have the time, you might enjoy enrolling in a class that would enhance your invitation-creation abilities. Many stationers offer in-house wedding invitation workshops that offer education with regards to paper and printing options, while others even provide the actual materials and instruction to achieve the finished product. As mentioned previously, many calligraphers and calligraphy societies offer basic calligraphy courses. If papermaking and the printing process are of interest to you, seek out your local book arts society, an art school, or an independent press to learn these skills yourself. Letterpress printing courses, in particular, are widely available and you may be able to use the facility's press to produce your own work.

Be sure to keep at least one pristine example of your invitation as a keepsake. >

Mr. and Mrs. William Prengaman
3535 Ridgewood Drive
Pittsburgh, Pennsylvania
15235

FINAL DETAILS

before you is a box of crisp, pristine papers. Inscribed with the names of you and your betrothed, they are waiting to share their message with your loved ones and friends. Congratulations, your invitations are ready! Take a moment to revel in their loveliness, and then it's time to get back to business—you still have a few tasks to complete to finish the job. Each envelope will need to be addressed and consequently filled with an invitation and its respective enclosures. Next, you will need to determine and apply the correct postage, and make a final trip to the post office to send your invitations on their merry way. After that, you can sit back and eagerly await the exciting responses of your guests as you count down the remaining days till you tie the knot.

page 114 Envelopes addressed in the bride's own handwriting are perhaps the most personal.

addressing the envelopes

Befitting such a momentous occasion, it is customary that guests' names and addresses be written on the envelopes in ink by hand, either via neat handwriting or stylized calligraphy. You may choose to do the honors yourself or enlist the aid of a talented friend or relative to scribe the envelopes for you as a wedding gift. If your budget allows, you might opt to hand off your envelopes to a professional calligrapher. Etiquette decrees that computer-generated adhesive address labels should never appear on any wedding invitation, however machine-generated calligraphy applied directly on envelopes has recently gained some acceptability. Regardless of which method you choose to get the job done, know that envelopes are always addressed unfilled with no postage applied. The most formal or traditional invitations are usually addressed in black or charcoal-gray ink. With less formal or contemporary invitations you can experiment with color, maybe choosing the same color ink to address the envelopes as used to print the invitations.

VIA YOUR OWN HAND If you or a friend possess good penmanship or a unique handwriting style suitable for the level of formality of your wedding, it is perfectly acceptable to take on the task of addressing the envelopes yourself. In fact, there is something heartfelt and charming about a bride lovingly writing out each guest's name and address simply in her own hand. Addressing your invitations yourself is also the most budget-friendly option.

Those who have the time and the artistic inclination may even wish to consult a calligraphy book or take a class from a professional calligrapher, local college, or art center. Italic is a manageable style to try as a beginner, and Copperplate script is a good choice for more artistic types and those not intimidated by using a dip pen and ink. A few words of caution: Don't take on this extra responsibility if it will add stress as your wedding date approaches, and, as always, be realistic in your expectations. Know that you won't be able to completely master traditional calligraphy hands with the skill of a professional (their art takes years to perfect), but the basic techniques you learn may give your own writing a more decorative flourish.

Wondering how to make sure each address line is straight? Some fine stationers provide a guide for you to use with your envelopes. If yours doesn't or if you have created your invitations yourself, you can use a trick of the professionals if your envelopes are unlined. Buy a photographer's light box (these are relatively inexpensive and available at most photography or art supply stores) then tape a ruled piece of paper to the box and place the envelope over it. When the box is lit, you'll be able to see the guidelines through the semi-transparent envelope. If you don't have a light box, you can also insert a piece of heavily ruled cardstock inside unlined envelopes to follow line by line. A piece of cardboard taped to a light box or your tabletop can also act as a little "shelf" to prevent the envelope from slipping as you write. If you have selected opaque or lined envelopes you will not be able to take advantage of these techniques; in these instances, use a ruler to guide you along each line or create a cardstock template to hold on top of the envelope as you write. You can draw guidelines lightly in soft-leaded pencil directly on the envelopes and erase them later with a white or light-colored eraser, however some calligraphers don't recommend doing this as ink can sometimes smear and ruin expensive wedding stationery.

Before deciding on your writing instrument, be sure to test out different pens on a sample of your actual envelopes; you never know how the ink might feather or how the pen tip might respond to the paper. When you're ready to begin try several practice runs, first on some plain envelopes and then once you feel comfortable you can address one of your actual envelopes. Keep a sufficient supply of extras on hand so you can correct mistakes once you get going. Work slowly and carefully at a time of day when you are relaxed and not rushed for best results. Allow about two weeks for addressing your envelopes if you are doing it yourself.

VIA THE HAND OF A PROFESSIONAL Fine hand calligraphy possesses an unmistakable beauty, from the look and feel of the ink on the paper to the signature swirls and flourishes applied to each letter by the calligrapher. A professional calligrapher not only relieves you of the responsibility of addressing the envelopes, but his or her work also presents a memorable first impression to your guests and makes them feel special when they see their names penned so handsomely. If you are leaning toward hiring a professional for your envelopes, you'll need to make the decision to do so about six months prior to your wedding date to allow enough time to research calligraphers, choose one, and book his or her services no less than four months in advance of your date (even though the actual task of addressing the envelopes need not happen until a couple of months before your wedding). It is not unusual for an in-demand calligrapher to require a deposit of up to fifty percent to hold a space on the calendar for you.

The process for finding and hiring a calligrapher to address your envelopes is essentially the same for finding and hiring an invitation calligrapher (see page 74). Before you start contacting calligraphers, assess your budget and needs (i.e. addressing outer envelopes only, or addressing outer and inner envelopes plus seating cards, place cards, and so forth), know approximately how many invitations will need to be addressed (remember that this number does not equal the number of guests you are inviting) and have a sense of the style of calligraphy you like (i.e. italic versus script versus artful handwriting; see page 76 for examples). Narrow your search down to one or two calligraphers and arrange to meet in person to take a look at their work or ask if they will send you samples or write an envelope for you. When reviewing a calligrapher's envelope samples, pay attention to the flow of the letters and the line spacing, and look for a balanced layout. The lettering should be relatively uniform, and the address lines should be straight and even. However, remember that calligraphy is created by hand, after all, and certain imperfections are part of the appeal. The actual lines of the address as written on the envelope may be staggered and indented, centered, or flush to the left. You can also request to have the zip code on its own line beneath the city and state; the numbers can be spread evenly from the left to right

Guests might be inclined to cherish an envelope exquisitely calligraphed in flourished >
copperplate as a keepsake—it's not often that mail so lovely arrives in your box!

Mr. and Mrs. Adam McPhee
Five Lighthouse Lane
Cape Elizabeth, Maine
04107

borders of the city and state line for a stylish statement. See if your calligrapher has samples of each of these variations so you can choose.

Regarding rates, some calligraphers will charge by the individual envelope or item, some offer one charge for an ensemble (i.e. both outer and inner envelopes as well as return address flaps), and some charge by the individual line. Understand a calligrapher's position on this topic as the price can vary greatly. Fees will also vary based on a calligrapher's experience. Many aspects impact a calligrapher's addressing costs, including the level of difficulty of the style you have selected (more complicated styles can take a calligrapher a longer time to create), whether or not your envelopes are lined (unlined or lined in tissue are preferred; opaque linings require a more difficult and time-consuming process to address), if you have requested a colored or color-matched ink, and how quickly you need the calligraphy completed.

As far as calligraphy style is concerned, you will want to show (or at the very least, discuss) a sample of your invitation or the font you have selected to your calligrapher as well as the envelope you intend to use. Whether a formal copperplate script or a more contemporary handwriting style, it is desirable for the writing on the envelope to coordinate with or complement what's inside on the invitation. Many of the same hands used to create a calligraphed invitation (see page 76) can be used for addressing. Often calligraphers can match the writing to an engraved or printed invitation font (some of which are originally based on handwriting in the first place), while other calligraphers have developed their own special hands. If you don't see the style you want in a calligrapher's repertoire, find someone else who can do it; the nuances of certain hands aren't learned overnight, and you don't want your envelopes to be a calligrapher's first attempt at a style he or she has never done before.

Be aware that the type of paper used to create your invitation envelopes will have some bearing on the outcome of the calligraphy. For even the most experienced calligrapher, papers that are handmade or very porous or textured are a challenge (if not an impossibility) as they can catch the nib of the pen and produce less than optimal results. In addition, papers in dark colors or those that are glossy, coated, pearlized, metallic, or have some other finish may simply not take ink well. Occasionally, envelopes with the return address printed via thermography may make calligraphy difficult if some of the thermography residue transfers to the face of a neighboring envelope. If you are absolutely certain you will want calligraphy on your envelopes, your best bet when selecting your invitations is to choose one with an envelope crafted of one hundred percent cotton with a smooth finish. Understand, too, that the size or shape of your envelope may limit your options; a looping embellished script might not be the best choice for a small or narrow envelope. Likewise, if a large portion of your guest list has very long last names or addresses, a simpler calligraphy style may be most feasible.

Once you've selected your calligrapher and ironed out all the details, you will need to communicate the information for your envelopes. Brush up on suggested envelope wording (see page 45) and complete a typed—

POINTS FOR THE CALLIGRAPHER'S CONTRACT

While a written recap of the details of your agreement is ideal, many calligraphers are not accustomed to working with a formal contract. It is helpful to discuss and outline the following important points, even simply via email, to make sure you are both clear on dates and deliverables for both sides:

- Calligraphy style selected
- Ink color
- Items (i.e. outer envelopes, place cards, etc.) requiring calligraphy and number of each
- Pricing
- Additional charges (extra lines of type, colored ink, etc.)
- Policy for mistakes, re-dos, late-stage additions
- Preferred guestlist format for outer envelope and inner envelope (as well as seating cards, table cards, and place cards); date due to calligrapher from bride
- Number of extra envelopes required and date due to calligrapher from bride
- Arrangements for pick up and delivery of work
- Method of payment and terms
- Sales tax or delivery charges if applicable
- Project deadline
- Total amount due and record of any deposit amount paid

not handwritten—list of your guests' names and addresses. Spend time putting your list together carefully, and check and double check the information to avoid costly mistakes on your part. The information should be written exactly as you would like it to appear, and should be as complete and correct as humanly possible before sending it to your calligrapher. He or she may request this list be delivered in a particular format (be sure to inquire), but in general the list should be easy to understand and read and should include:

- Upper and lower case letters in a standard font and large point size for readability
- Titles for all individuals
- All information such as Street, Avenue, Apartment, and so forth spelled out
- Five-digit zip codes

If you have both outer and inner envelopes, a two-column format is useful:

OUTER ENVELOPE	INNER ENVELOPE
Mr. and Mrs. Stephen Reynolds	Mr. & Mrs. Reynolds
1621 Lexington Avenue	*or a less formal version of*
Apartment 7D	*their names if appropriate*
New York, New York	*(i.e. Uncle Stephen and Aunt Ella)*
10016	Charles and Maureen*
	when the couple has children
	you'd like to invite too

Add a third column for spouses' names should your calligrapher also be preparing place cards for you.

Put your name, contact information and wedding date at the top of every page, and number each address and each page so that you and the calligrapher can cross reference easily if need be. And, it probably goes without saying, but remember to make an extra copy for yourself. Discuss with your calligrapher how many extra envelopes he or she would like; be prepared to provide ten to twenty percent more than the actual number of invitations you have to allow for rewrites and corrections.

Once the calligrapher has all of your materials, you can expect the actual turnaround time to address one hundred envelopes to be about two to four weeks depending on the style you have selected and whether it is "high wedding season" (generally April through October). A good calligrapher will proofread his or her work against your typed list, so mistakes will be rare. However, once you receive your envelopes immediately review them yourself against your list for spelling errors, transposed numbers, and the like. If the calligrapher has in fact made a mistake, let him or her know and expect the change to be made free of charge. If you realize you made the error on your typed guest list and the calligrapher simply repeated your mistake, expect to pay a re-do fee. Once the calligrapher has completed the original assignment, you may find yourself with some late additions—either guests you forgot to include or new guests from a second round of invitations off your B-list. Try to submit any and all additions at one time; some calligraphers will gladly accommodate add-ons a one-time request, but after that your job is considered done and you may need to pay an extra charge should you find you have more additions later and your calligrapher has to interrupt another commission to accommodate you.

VIA MACHINE If you cannot write your envelopes yourself and the cost of a calligrapher doesn't work within your overall invitation budget, there is a relatively new addressing alternative called machine calligraphy (also known as computer or digital calligraphy) that you may want to try. In this technique, computerized fonts have been developed to mimic the hands written by calligraphers and classic engraving fonts, and envelopes are passed through printers, which apply the type directly to the paper. Letters are perfectly uniform and in straight lines, creating a neat, consistent—albeit somewhat flat—appearance on your envelopes. While nothing can replace the fluid beauty and soul of a handwritten address, the quality of some machine calligraphy can be quite good, and the process has generally become more acceptable for semi-formal and informal invitations (since strict wedding etiquette frowns on anything other than written envelopes, it is still best to arrange for handwriting or calligraphy for formal invitations).

Even though the result is not exactly the same as true hand calligraphy, machine calligraphy may also be affected by similar factors, such as the type of paper your envelope is crafted from (which may or may not take ink well) and the envelope's size (certain machine calligraphy fonts do not look good sized down for smaller envelopes). It is a good idea to arrange to forward a sample of your envelope to any companies you may be considering to determine whether or not their printing method will take to the envelope paper and to see actual results for yourself. You will also need to communicate your guest information in some way, so check if a company has a preferred format for delivery and review the suggestions on page 123. And just as you would with a hand calligrapher, be sure to proof the finished envelopes against your original list upon arrival to guard against errors.

If you purchased your invitations from a stationer or worked with a wedding planner, they can probably recommend a reliable machine calligrapher. Many stationers offer their own services on-site. Or, you can search the internet to find a machine calligraphy business and browse their offerings online. It is not necessary to find someone local; you may ship your envelopes to a machine calligrapher (or hand calligrapher, for that matter)

SHIPPING YOUR ENVELOPES

If you have decided to have your envelopes calligraphed by hand or by machine, you may need to pack them up and send them off somewhere for the work to be done. It pays to take extra care when preparing your envelope packaging. Here are some tips to follow to ensure your envelopes arrive at their destination without looking like they've already been through the mail.

- Ship your envelopes in a sturdy cardboard box, not the original stationery box or a padded envelope.
- Place loose envelopes in resealable plastic bags to protect them from dirt and moisture.
- Wrap the bags of envelopes with bubble wrap or surround them with packing peanuts; they should not be able to move around inside the shipping box.

anywhere in the country. Some companies will do everything for you, from typing up your guest list to printing and stuffing your envelopes (certain calligraphers are willing to do this as well). Others offer a more hands-on approach and allow you to type in your own guest information yourself online. Many machine calligraphy companies offer hundreds of different type choices in classic calligraphy and script fonts as well as contemporary handwriting styles, and they may even incorporate artwork or monograms along with the addressing.

As with other invitation professionals, quality can vary. The range of machine calligraphy companies includes everything from startups with laser printers to seasoned specialists using patented wet-ink processes, so be sure to review actual samples and contact references to find the most reputable sources. If no contract is provided, review the important general points on page

124 with your sales person. Many companies post their purchase, return, and re-do policies online; always read any fine print carefully to avoid any misunderstandings. Machine calligraphy averages about half the price of traditional hand calligraphy and generally takes about a week or so to complete.

If you'd still prefer to do the addressing yourself but need help in the penmanship department, software which translates your handwriting into the fluid curves of common calligraphy hands is also available online for you to use on your own computer.

assembling the invitations

All addressed up and ready to go? Unless your stationer, calligrapher, or wedding planner has already done the deed, you'll need to assemble all your invitation elements and prepare to fill the envelopes. For those with large guest lists or lots of information to disseminate, this can be a pretty big job. If you are doing it yourself, make a party of it to lighten your load and ask your bridesmaids to get together one afternoon to help you. Or, spend some quality pre-wedding time with your mother or future mother-in-law or future husband to get the job done.

FIRST THINGS FIRST If you are using reply cards, take a sample down to the post office to determine necessary postage and purchase the correct amount (to save time, get your fully stuffed invitation weighed now, too). Don't forget to subtract the number of reply cards that will be mailed to guests in foreign countries, because those invited guests will have to purchase and apply their native postage to the reply cards. Next separate your outer envelopes into two groups if need be: those who get enclosures (such as out-of-towners) and those who don't. Then, lay out all your elements in neat piles, assembly-line style, and collect each piece in the correct order as described below.

WHAT GOES WHERE The stacking order of all the elements of your invitation is pretty straightforward, and generally follows in size from the smallest piece on the top (usually the reply card and its envelope) to the largest on the bottom (the invitation itself). If you are using an inner envelope, the invitation and all of its elements are placed inside and face the envelope's back with their left edges along the inside bottom of the envelope. The stuffed inner envelope is placed, unsealed, into the outer envelope with its face facing the back of the outer envelope (the recipient would be able to immediately read his or her name when removing the inner envelope from the outer envelope with the right hand. If you have elected to forgo the inner envelope, you still follow the same stacking order for the elements.

The classic assembly order is, from the top:

- face-up reply card tucked underneath the flap of the face down reply envelope
- reception card
- invitation (if single card or single fold style)

Any tissues, should they be provided and should you decide to use them, are to be placed wherever there is printed text (for example, on top of the

Once the response card, reception card, and invitation are safely tucked inside, >
leave the inner envelope unsealed and place it face up into the outer envelope.

700 Park Avenue
New York, New York 10021

OUTER ENVELOPE

INNER ENVELOPE

at *the* *daughter*

Andr*ew* *Marshall*

to

INVITATION

Mr. Jonathan Wilton Briggs III

on Saturday, the seventh of June

at eleven o'clock

TISSUE

Saint James' Church

Madison Avenue at 7*1st* Street

New York City

RECEPTION CARD Reception

immediately following the ceremony

The Carlyle

REPLY CARD AND ENVELOPE

is reque*sted by the* twentieth

M_____

will_____attend

invitation, the reception card, and the reply card). Other elements such as maps, direction cards, and accommodation cards should be inserted face up into the pile according to size. One exception to the norm: If you have a french-fold invitation, all of the enclosures are inserted face up within the invitation as opposed to being placed on top of it. You can always tell whether you have filled an envelope correctly by examining the way the elements sit within: If you were to remove the stack with your right hand, would you immediately be able to read the type? If the answer is yes, you've done it right!

SEALED WITH A KISS As much as you love your invitations, chances are you don't want to lick all of the envelope flaps. Make haste to a stationery store, where you'll discover plenty of sealing tools. If you want, fashion your own device by attaching a clothespin or binder clip to small square of sponge and use it with a shallow bowl of water (just be sure to keep the bowl far away from your pile of stuffed invitations). Once an envelope has been sealed, allow it to dry flap-side-up on a table for a few minutes before stacking it on top of another envelope to prevent smearing the name and address of its neighbor. Your sealing tool can also come in handy when it's time to adhere stamps to your invitations.

mailing the invitations

As mentioned previously, standard procedure is to post wedding invitations six to eight weeks before the big day. If you are having a destination wedding, are expecting a fair number of out of town guests, or are marrying on or near a holiday, you may wish to push your mailing date back to ten to twelve weeks before your wedding.

While you may never have been to Romance, Arkansas, your invitations can easily make the trip and receive a charming postmark as a souvenir to prove it to your guests. The post offices of these actual towns in the United States will gladly mark your stamped envelopes with their appropriately-monikered names. Simply pack your stuffed, sealed, stamped invitations well in a box (follow the tips on page 128), and include a letter requesting the invitations be hand-cancelled with the town's postmark and mailed. Address your box to:

> Postmaster
> Town, State
> Zip Code

Make sure to phone ahead to alert the post office of your precious package's imminent arrival and ship the box via a trackable service. Check with the postmaster, but a window of about two weeks should be enough for the invitations to be delivered, postmarked, and mailed.

Bliss, ID 83314	Honey Grove, PA 17035	Luck, WI 54853
Bliss, NY 14024	Honey Grove, TX 75446	Paradise, CA 95967
Bond, Co 80423	Honeyville, UT 84314	Romance, AR 72136
Bridal Veil, OR 97010	Hope, AK 64870	Romeo, CO 81148
Chapel Hill, NC 27514	Kissimmee, FL 34744	Romeo, MI 48065
Darling, MS 38623	Lovejoy, GA 30250	Sugar City, CO 81076
Deary, ID 83823	Lovejoy, IL 62059	Sugar City, ID 83448
Diamond, Ok 97722	Lovelady, TX 75851	Sweet, ID 83670
Eros, LA 71238	Loveland, CO 80538	Union, IL 17803
Groom, TX 79039	Loveland, OH 45140	Union, IA 50258
Harmony, RI 02829	Loveland, OK 73553	Union, KY 41091
Heart Butte, MT 59448	Lovely, KY 41231	Valentine, NE 69201
Heartwell, NE 68945	Loveville, MD 20656	Valentines, VA 23887
Honey Brook, PA 19344	Loving, NM 88256	Venus, FL 33960
Honey Creek, WI 53138	Loving, TX 76460	Venus, PA 16364

POSTAGE, PLEASE   Proper postage is, of course, required. If you haven't already, bring a sample of your complete, stuffed invitation to your local post office to be weighed. If different guests are getting different invitations (for example, only traveling guests are receiving additional enclosures with information about airlines and accommodations), be sure to bring every complete permutation along and get them weighed separately. Keep in mind that unusually large and different shaped envelopes (even squares) are subject to additional postage.

When purchasing stamps, view them as another opportunity to personalize your wedding invitation. You can't go wrong with the "Love" stamp, which has been specifically designed with standard two-ounce wedding invitations in mind (a companion one-ounce "Love" stamp can coordinate your reply card envelopes). However, if your particular invitation requires additional postage, you may wish to choose stamps with a meaningful image or colors that complement your invitation. Inquire of your local postmaster what's currently available, or browse a wide selection online at www.usps.com. One unbreakable rule: This is not a mass mailing from a direct marketing company or business—under no circumstances should you use a postal meter for your invitations or reply card envelopes.

REQUEST TO CANCEL   These days, everyday mail is whisked through postal machinery that marks each piece with a delivery bar code and occasionally an in-house advertisement of our nation's postal services. As you

Details like meaningful postmarks and beautiful postage make all the difference > between a common invitation and one that feels special.

know, your wedding invitations are no mere pieces of ordinary mail. You can keep their faces blemish free by bringing the whole lot to the post office and requesting hand-canceling. With this old fashioned procedure, your postal clerk will neatly ink only the stamp on each piece by hand.

paper of your own

One final note, so to speak, concerns social stationery to be used for thank you notes or letters once you have married. Such stationery, either as sheets of paper or flat or folded cards, can be personalized in a variety of ways— a single initial monogram of the last name you now have in common, both sets of your initials if you have maintained your maiden name, both of your first names, or stationery just for you featuring your new married name. You might wish to order social stationery at the same time you order your wedding invitations, so you can continue to utilize a motif or color theme and perhaps the same printing method. Of course there are plenty of lovely commercial options out there, but your own special stationery will continue to convey the inimitable shared sense of style you debuted with your wedding invitation.

something to remember

Long after your wedding is over, you'll have many tangible remembrances of your day—a ring on your finger, a gown in your closet, and of course your spouse at your side. Too often, the wedding invitation may be lost somewhere in the shuffle, tossed in a drawer or tucked away in a box in the attic. Since you gave your invitation so much thought while creating it, why not give it some pride of place and transform it into a keepsake? You may wish to buy a pretty frame and hang your invitation somewhere in your new home together. An inexpensive shadow box provides an elegant forum for displaying your invitation and other paper ephemera such as a program and your two reception place cards. For an heirloom-quality memento, a fine jeweler can replicate your exact wedding invitation in a small sterling silver tray. Or, use the engraver's plate from your invitation as a desk paperweight as a day to day reminder of your wedding.

MR. AND MRS. WILLIAM STRATTON
REQUEST THE HONOR OF YOUR PRESENCE
AT THE MARRIAGE OF THEIR DAUGHTER

CHARLOTTE ALEXANDRA
· TO ·
DUNCAN ANDREW MACDONALD

SATURDAY, THE SIXTEENTH OF OCTOBER
TWO THOUSAND AND TWO
AT HALF AFTER FIVE O'CLOCK
GREEN GATE FARM
AQUINNAH, MASSACHUSETTS

· · ·

 APPENDIX

CHECKLIST AND TIMELINE

Use this general timeline as a checklist and to make sure you stay on schedule. Of course, not every item here may apply to you. Most wedding experts advise the overall process of choosing and creating your invitations (not counting assembling, addressing, and mailing) takes somewhere in the neighborhood of six to eight months.

1 YEAR

- Get engaged!
- Set a wedding date
- Compile a guest list
- Book ceremony and reception sites
- Far-flung destination weddings: send out save-the-date cards

9 MONTHS

- Start researching invitation styles you like; build an idea file
- Plot out potential invitation wording; review with all interested parties
- Consider what, if any, enclosures you might need

7 TO 8 MONTHS

- Decide on a creation method (stationer, do it yourself, etc.)
- Choose and order/create save-the-date cards

6 MONTHS

- Meet with stationer/ designer/calligrapher to discuss invitation creation
- Local weddings: Mail save-the-date cards

5 MONTHS

- Finalize invitation style and wording
- Create/order your invitations
- Book a calligrapher to address envelopes

4 MONTHS

- Review your proof
- Receive your invitations and envelopes
- Create typed list of guests' names and addresses

3 MONTHS

- Address the envelopes (allow 2-4 weeks)
- Weigh complete invitation and individual reply card with envelope at post office; buy postage

10 WEEKS

- Assemble and seal invitations
- Apply postage
- Destination weddings: request hand-cancelling at post office and mail invitations
- Specialized postmarks: contact post office and ship invitations (allow 2 weeks)

8 WEEKS

- Local weddings: request hand-cancelling at post office and mail invitations

4 WEEKS

- Last call to send out B-list invitations
- Mail rehearsal dinner invitations
- Mail postwedding brunch invitations

2 WEEKS

- Contact guests who have not rsvp'd
- Submit final head count and seating chart to caterer and/or wedding planner
- Create table cards and place cards

THE BIG DAY

Have a wonderful time!

INVITATION AND ENVELOPE WORDING

Wording seems to cause brides and grooms the most grief when it comes to wedding invitations. Traditional wording is very formulaic, so if yours is this type of wedding all you need to do is reference the following examples and put in your own information as appropriate. Examples of contemporary wording are also included; you may wish to alter this wording as you like, just make sure your verbiage reflects the solemnity of your particular occasion.

CEREMONY INVITATIONS

TRADITIONAL WORDING EXAMPLES

BRIDE'S MARRIED PARENTS HOST
Mr. and Mrs. Robert Wright Richter
request the honour of your presence
at the marriage of their daughter
Gillian Eloise
to
Mr. James Francis Frasier
Saturday, the tenth of August
Two thousand and nine
at four o'clock
Church of Saint Stephen
Baltimore, Maryland

BRIDE'S MARRIED PARENTS HOST;
MOTHER HAS RETAINED MAIDEN NAME
Ellen Marie Rodale
and Robert Wright Richter
request the honour of your presence
at the marriage of their daughter
Gillian Eloise
to
Mr. James Francis Frasier
Saturday, the tenth of August
Two thousand and nine
at four o'clock
Church of Saint Stephen
Baltimore, Maryland

BRIDE'S DIVORCED PARENTS HOST;
MOTHER NOT REMARRIED
Mrs. Ellen Rodale Richter
Mr. Robert Wright Richter
request the honour of your presence
at the marriage of their daughter
Gillian Eloise
to
Mr. James Francis Frasier
Saturday, the tenth of August
Two thousand and nine
at four o'clock
Church of Saint Stephen
Baltimore, Maryland

BRIDE'S DIVORCED NOT REMARRIED
MOTHER HOSTS
Mrs. Ellen Rodale Richter *or* Ms. Ellen Rodale
requests the honor of your presence
at the marriage of her daughter
Gillian Eloise Richter
to
Mr. James Francis Frasier
Saturday, the tenth of August
Two thousand and nine
at four o'clock
Church of Saint Stephen
Baltimore, Maryland

BRIDE'S DIVORCED PARENTS HOST;
MOTHER REVERTED TO MAIDEN NAME
Ellen Marie Rodale
Robert Wright Richter
request the honour of your presence
at the marriage of their daughter
Gillian Eloise
to
Mr. James Francis Frasier
Saturday, the tenth of August
Two thousand and nine
at four o'clock
Church of Saint Stephen
Baltimore, Maryland

BRIDE'S DIVORCED PARENTS HOST;
MOTHER HAS REMARRIED

Mrs. Edward Thomas Sloan
Mr. Robert Wright Richter
request the honour of your presence
at the marriage of their daughter
Gillian Eloise
to
Mr. James Francis Frasier
Saturday, the tenth of August
Two thousand and nine
at four o'clock
Church of Saint Stephen
Baltimore, Maryland

BRIDE'S DIVORCED AND REMARRIED
PARENTS COHOST

Mr. and Mrs. Edward Thomas Sloan
and
Mr. and Mrs. Robert Wright Richter
request the honor of your presence
at the marriage of
Gillian Eloise Richter
to
Mr. James Francis Frasier
Saturday, the tenth of August
Two thousand and nine
at four o'clock
Church of Saint Stephen
Baltimore, Maryland

BRIDE'S REMARRIED MOTHER AND
HUSBAND HOST

Mr. and Mrs. Edward Thomas Sloan
request the honor of your presence
at the marriage of Mrs. Sloan's daughter
Gillian Eloise Richter
to
Mr. James Francis Frasier
Saturday, the tenth of August
Two thousand and nine
at four o'clock
Church of Saint Stephen
Baltimore, Maryland

BRIDE'S WIDOWED MOTHER/FATHER HOSTS

Only the surviving parent is listed on the invitation

Mr./Mrs. Robert Wright Richter
requests the honor of your presence
at the marriage of his/her daughter
Gillian Eloise
to
Mr. James Francis Frasier
Saturday, the tenth of August
Two thousand and nine
at four o'clock
Church of Saint Stephen
Baltimore, Maryland

BRIDE'S MARRIED PARENTS HOST;
GROOM'S MARRIED PARENTS
ACKNOWLEDGED*
Mr. and Mrs. Robert Wright Richter
request the honour of your presence
at the marriage of their daughter
Gillian Eloise
to
Mr. James Francis Frasier
son of
Mr. and Mrs. Marc Ellis Frasier
Saturday, the tenth of August
Two thousand and nine
at four o'clock
Church of Saint Stephen
Baltimore, Maryland

*NOTE: This would also be the format for an
invitation to a Jewish wedding, with "to"
replaced by "and" along with the name
of the temple.

GROOM'S MARRIED PARENTS HOST
Mr. and Mrs. Marc Ellis Frasier
request the honour of your presence
at the marriage of
Miss Gillian Eloise Richter
to their son
James Francis Frasier
Saturday, the tenth of August
Two thousand and nine
at four o'clock
Church of Saint Stephen
Baltimore, Maryland

BOTH SETS OF MARRIED PARENTS HOST
Mr. and Mrs. Robert Wright Richter
and
Mr. and Mrs. Marc Ellis Frasier
request the honour of your presence
at the marriage of their children
Gillian Eloise Richter
and
James Francis Frasier
Saturday, the tenth of August
Two thousand and nine
at four o'clock
Church of Saint Stephen
Baltimore, Maryland

BRIDE AND GROOM HOST
Version I
The honour of your presence
is requested at the marriage of
Miss Gillian Eloise Richter
to
Mr. James Francis Frasier
Saturday, the tenth of August
Two thousand and nine
at four o'clock
Church of Saint Stephen
Baltimore, Maryland

Version II
Miss Gillian Eloise Richter
and
Mr. James Francis Frasier
request the honour of your presence
at their marriage
Saturday, the tenth of August
Two thousand and nine
at four o'clock
Church of Saint Stephen
Baltimore, Maryland

CONTEMPORARY WORDING EXAMPLES

Version I
Together with their families,
Gillian Eloise Richter
and
James Francis Frasier
invite you to share in their joy
as they are wed
Saturday, the tenth of August
Two thousand and nine
at four o'clock
Church of Saint Stephen
Baltimore, Maryland

Version II
On this day, two become one
Gillian Eloise Richter
and
James Francis Frasier
invite you to witness their marriage
Saturday, the tenth of August
Two thousand and nine
at four o'clock
Church of Saint Stephen
Baltimore, Maryland

Version III
Please join
Gillian Eloise Richter
and
James Francis Frasier
as they celebrate their marriage
Saturday, the tenth of August
Two thousand and nine
at four o'clock
Church of Saint Stephen
Baltimore, Maryland

LOCATION VARIATIONS

WEDDING AT HOME
Mr. and Mrs. Robert Wright Richter
request the pleasure of your company
at the marriage of their daughter
Gillian Eloise
to
Mr. James Francis Frasier
Saturday, the tenth of August
Two thousand and nine
at four o'clock
142 Scottswood Road
Riverside, Illinois

WEDDING AT A RESIDENCE
OTHER THAN THE HOSTS'
Mr. and Mrs. Robert Wright Richter
request the pleasure of your company
at the marriage of their daughter
Gillian Eloise
to
Mr. James Francis Frasier
Saturday, the tenth of August
Two thousand and nine
at four o'clock
at the residence of
Mr. and Mrs. Jordan Lucas Allston
566 Red Farm Road
Great Barrington, Massachusetts

CEREMONY AND RECEPTION INVITATION
BOTH EVENTS AT SAME LOCATION
Mr. and Mrs. Robert Wright Richter
request the honour of your presence
at the marriage of their daughter
Gillian Eloise
to
Mr. James Francis Frasier
Saturday, the tenth of August
Two thousand and nine
at four o'clock
The University Club
San Francisco, CA
and afterwards at the reception

EVENTS AT SEPARATE LOCATIONS
Mr. and Mrs. Robert Wright Richter
request the honour of your presence
at the marriage of their daughter
Gillian Eloise
to
Mr. James Francis Frasier
Saturday, the tenth of August
Two thousand and nine
at four o'clock
Church of Saint Stephen
Baltimore, Maryland
Reception immediately following
Rolling Greens Country Club
Towson, Maryland

RECEPTION INVITATION

Mr. and Mrs. Robert Wright Richter
request the pleasure of your company
at the wedding reception for their daughter
Gillian Eloise
and
Mr. James Francis Frasier
Saturday, the tenth of August
Two thousand and nine
at six o'clock
Rolling Greens Country Club
Towson, Maryland

RECEPTION CARD

Reception immediately following
the ceremony
Rolling Greens Country Club
Towson, Maryland

CEREMONY CARD

The honour of your presence is requested
at the marriage ceremony
Saturday, the tenth of August
Two thousand and nine
at four o'clock
Church of Saint Stephen
Baltimore, Maryland

RESPONSE CARD

Version I
M_____
will_____attend

The favor of a reply is requested before
the fifteenth of July

Version II
M_____
_____will attend
_____will not attend

The favor of a reply is requested before
the fifteenth of July

Version III
The favor of a reply is requested by July 15th
M_____
accepts_____
regrets_____

ENCLOSURES

ADMISSION CARD

Version I
Please present this card
at the Church of Saint Stephen
Baltimore, Maryland

Version II (formal)
[Mr. and Mrs. William Robinson] *handwritten*
will please present this card
at the Church of Saint Stephen
Baltimore, Maryland

RESERVED SEATING CARDS

Pew card
Please present this card
at the Church of Saint Stephen
Saturday, the tenth of August
Pew number: _____

Within the ribbon
Within the ribbon

AT HOME CARD

Version I
At home
after September first
2500 North Lake Shore Drive
Chicago, Illinois 60614
(312) 788-3989

Version II
Mr. and Mrs. James Frasier
will be at home
after September first
2500 North Lake Shore Drive
Chicago, Illinois 60614
(312) 788-3989

Version III
Gillian Richter and James Frasier
will be at home
after September first
2500 North Lake Shore Drive
Chicago, Illinois 60614
(312) 788-3989

ACCOMMODATIONS CARD

Accommodations
Maple Tree Inn
(305) 594-3600

Ritz Carlton
(305) 594-7500

PARKING CARD

Complimentary parking is provided
Astor Parking Garage
1102 W. Ashland Avenue
Please present this card to attendant;
fees and gratuities included

TRANSPORTATION CARD

Version I
Transportation will be provided from
the ceremony to the reception

Version II
A trolley will be available in front of the
Maple Leaf Inn at half past three o'clock
to transport guests to the ceremony.
The trolley will also transport guests from
the ceremony to the reception, then back to
the inn at the end of the evening.

THE OUTER AND INNER ENVELOPES

	OUTER ENVELOPE	INNER ENVELOPE
Single man	Mr. Gerald Thomas	Mr. Thomas (or Gerald if you know the person intimately)
Single woman	Miss or Ms. Jean Price	Miss or Ms. Price
Single person with guest	Mr. Gerald Thomas	Mr. Thomas and guest
	Miss or Ms. Jean Price	Miss or Ms. Price and guest
Married couple	Mr. and Mrs. Gerald Thomas	Mr. and Mrs. Thomas
Married couple, different surnames	Ms. Jean Price and Mr. Gerald Thomas	Ms. Price and Mr. Thomas
Cohabitating couple	Miss or Ms. Jean Price Mr. Gerald Thomas	Miss or Ms. Price Mr. Thomas
Same sex couple (in alphabetical order)	Mr. Joseph Albertson Mr. Timothy Zane or Ms. Elizabeth Austen Ms. Margot Zento	Mr. Albertson Mr. Zane or Ms. Austen Ms. Zento
Family with children under 18 (in descending age order)	Mr. and Mrs. Gerald Thomas	Mr. and Mrs. Thomas Lucy, Charles, and Mimi
Same sex children 18+ at home (eldest first)	The Misses Thomas or The Misses Thomas	The Misses Thomas Miss Anna Thomas Miss Beth Thomas
	The Messrs. Thomas or The Messrs. Thomas	The Messrs. Thomas Mr. Alexander Thomas Mr. Michael Thomas
Different sex children 18+ at home	Miss Mallory Thomas Mr. Andrew Thomas	Miss Thomas Mr. Thomas

SOURCE GUIDE

INVITATION COMPANIES

Generally you can browse invitation designs on a company's website. Many of these companies only offer their products through approved retailers (usually the website provides a list by region), while others only provide custom work and collaborate with you directly.

Alpine Creative Group
www.alpineinvite.com
800-289-6507

Anna Griffin
www.annagriffin.com
404-817-8170

Arak Kanofsky Studios
www.arakkanofskystudios.com
610-599-1161

Bella Figura
www.bellafigura.com
315-473-0933

Bliss Ink
www.blissink.com
206-789-8069

Blue Moon Invitations
http://store.yahoo.com/
bluemooninvitations
inc/index.html
401-383-9078

Checkerboard Ltd.
www.checkerboardltd.com
800-735-2475

Claudia Calhoun
www.claudiacalhoun.com

Crane's
www.crane.com
800-268-2281

Dahlia Invites
www.dahliainvites.com
866-340-4440

Dauphinepress.com
www.dauphinepress.com
888-869-0659

Deckle Edge Design
www.deckledgedesign.com
212-794-8942

Dreamland Designs
www.dreamland-designs.com
612-341-2586

Eerie
www.eeriedesign.com
860-521-2668

Elum
www.elumdesigns.com
858-453-4500

Encore Studios
www.encorestudios.com
800-526-0497

Envelopments
www.envelopments.com
800-335-3536

InspirAsian Creations
www.inspirasiancreations.com
604-438-2466

Janel Claire Designs
www.janelclaire.com
510-601-6599

Julie Holcomb Printers
www.julieholcombprinters.com
510-654-6416

Lakehouse Design
www.lakehousedesign.com
978-594-0168

**Marc Friedland
Collection/Creative
Intelligence**
www.creative-intelligence.com
323-936-9009

Mia Carta Stationery
www.miacarta.com
617-541-0501

Mira Aster
www.miraaster.com
323-463-1252

Oblation
www.oblationpapers.com
503-223-1093

Page
www.atthepage.com

Pantry Press
www.pantrypress.net
800-511-4767

Paper Girl
www.paper-girl.com
626-818-5243

Papivore
www.papivore.com
printing@papivore.com

Real Card Studio
www.realcardstudio.com

Red Bliss
www.redbliss.com
603-679-5232

Red Ribbon Studio
www.redribbonstudio.com

Stacey Claire Boyd
www.staceyclaireboyd.com
205-324-4715

Stephannie Barba
www.stephanniebarba.com
415-437-6001

Studio Z
www.studio-z.com
707-964-9448

Stylepress
866-675-7895

William Arthur
www.williamarthur.com
custserv@williamarthur.com

Wren Press
www.wrenpress.com
212-249-3055

You're Invited
www.youreinvited.com
877-468-4834

You Send Me
www.yousendme.com
423-267-8683

STATIONERS

These retail and online businesses carry a wide range of invitation brands and/or wedding stationery needs.

Alphabetique
www.alphabetiquechicago.com
312-751-2920

The American Wedding Album
www.theamericanwedding.com
800-428-0379

Bridalcraft
www.bridalcraft.com
215-412-4919

Carlson Craft Wedding
Invitations
www.carslon-craft-wedding-
invitations.com
512-691-9771

Cartier
800-227-8437

Chelsea Paper
www.chelseapaper.com
888-407-2726

Dempsey & Carroll
www.dempseyandcarroll.com
800-444-4019

eInvite
www.einvite.com
888.346.8483

Fine Stationery
www.finestationery.com
888-808-3463

How Inviting
www.howinviting.com
949-306-2402

Invitation Consultants
www.invitationconsultants.com
888-381-4400

Kate's Paperie
www.katespaperie.com
212-941-9816

Mrs. John L. Strong
www.mrsstrong.com
212-838-3775

My Gatsby
www.mygatsby.com
888-997-7899

Paper & Ink
www.paper-and-ink.com
512-477-3362

Paperfection
www.paperfection.com
877-289-5812

The Paper Shop
www.papershop.com
407-644-8700

Paper Style
www.paperstyle.com
888-670-5300

Papyrus
www.papyrusonline.com

Rebecca Moss
www.rebeccamoss.com

Silberman/Brown
www.silbermanbrown.com
425-455-3665

Smythson of Bond Street
www.smythson.com
877-769-8476

Soolip Paperie & Press
www.soolip.com
310-360-0545

Tiffany & Co.
800-843-3269

Wedding Orders
www.weddingorders.com
800-364-6972

Wedding Tulle
www.weddingtulle.com
415-359-9707

Yes I Do!
Invitations & Fine Stationery
www.yesido.net
201-659-3300

Calligraphy by Nan Deluca
www.scribenyc.com
212-477-3732

Cambridge Calligraphy
www.cambridgecalligraphy.com
877-467-2214
machine-generated calligraphy

**Cynscribe Calligraphy
Directory**
www.cynscribe.com

Friends of Calligraphy
www.friendsofcalligraphy.org

Gail Brill Design
www.gailbrilldesign.com
518-891-0182

**Harriet Rose
Calligraphy & Design**
www.rosecalligraphy.com
212-663-4564

Maisner Calligraphy Studios
www.bernardmaisner.com
212-477-6776

Paperwhite Studio
www.paperwhitestudio.com
207-892-7815

Society for Calligraphy
www.societyforcalligraphy.com

Society of Scribes
www.societyofscribes.org

Stylish Addressing
www.stylishaddressing.com
210-520-3322
machine-generated calligraphy

**Washington
Calligraphers Guild**
www.calligraphersguild.org

PRINTING CLASSES

**Armory Center for the Arts,
Pasadena**
www.armoryarts.org
626-792-5101

The Book Arts Web
www.philobiblon.com

**The Center for Book Arts,
New York**
www.centerforbookarts.org
212-481-0295

**Otis College of Art and Design,
Los Angeles**
www.otis.edu
310-665-6800

OTHER RESOURCES

Briar Press
www.briarpress.org
dingbats

Chank Diesel
www.chank.com
unique fonts

Chey Design
www.cheydesign.com
chey@cheydesign.com
custom map design

Frame Your Day
www.frameyourday.com
920-362-6531
invitation preservation

**Claudia Hanlin's
Wedding Library**
www.theweddinglibrary.com
212-327-0100
wedding vendor resource and boutique

credits

INVITATIONS

Contact information for the following can be found in the Source Guide starting on page 151.
page 7: William Arthur; page 10: Kate's Custom Letterpress, Kate's Paperie; page 14: Papivore; page 17: Red Ribbon Studio; page 20: Crane's; page 26: Paperwhite Studio; page 31: Gail Brill Design; page 35: Stephanie Barba; page 36: How Inviting; page 44: Ecrie; page 49: Wedding Tulle; page 58: Lakehouse Design; page 62: Dempsey & Carroll; page 65: Julie Holcomb Printers; page 75: Oblation; page 76: script style samples by Paperwhite Studio; page 79: Envelopments; page 84: Gail Brill Design; page 87: Arak Kanofsky; page 88: Wedding Tulle; page 90: Paper Girl; page 99: Dreamland Designs; page 106: Snow & Graham; page 113: Anna Griffin; page 121: Paperwhite Studio; page 131: Dempsey & Carroll; page 138 and cover: Kate's Custom Letterpress, Kate's Paperie

PROPS
page 10: pin courtesy of Purl, 212-420-8796, www.purlsoho.com; pages 44 and 121: pins courtesy of Robin Richman, 773-278-6150, www.robinrichman.com

acknowledgments

There are several people to thank for their role in the creation of this book. First, thanks to all the wonderful invitation designers, printers, and stationers whose beautiful invitations appear on these pages. Thanks, too, to the artful hands of Gail Brill and Erica McPhee as well as fellow calligraphers Nan DeLuca, Anne Robin, and Harriet Rose for sharing their extensive knowledge and love of their craft. I also greatly appreciate the help of the people at Cranes, Julie Pauly and the staff of the renowned Kate's Paperie, Claudia Hanlin, and New York's Center for Book Arts.

A very special thanks to the thoughtful and brilliant Ivette Montes de Oca for introducing me to the folks at Stewart Tabori & Chang: Leslie Stoker, Sandy Gilbert, and of course my tireless, thorough, and trusty editor Beth Huseman. (I hope you find something you like in this book when you're ready to tie the knot!)

I am in awe of art director Amy Trombat's vision, and many, many thanks to photographer Dana Gallagher (skillfully assisted by Ellie Miller) for her beautiful imagery, hospitality, and making it all look so easy. I also tip my hat to our lovely stylist Kelly McKaig.

Big kiss to my talented circle of design friends who always seem to be able to answer any question at the drop of a hat: Mark DeMott, Elizabeth Irwin, Dimity Jones, Brittany O'Neil, Maribeth Romslo, and Anne Secor.

On the home front, thank you to my dear friend Kathy Lynch who wouldn't leave the printer till my own invitation was perfect, my parents Jan and Jerry Cegielski for always keeping me prominently displayed on their bookshelf, and my sweet husband Alan Tosler and delightful daughter Violet for the "family hugs" whenever I took a writing break.

Editor Beth Huseman
Designer Amy Trombat
Production Manager Jane Searle

Published in 2004 by
Stewart, Tabori & Chang
115 West 18th Street
New York, NY 10011

Canadian Distribution:
Canadian Manda Group
One Atlantic Avenue, Suite 105
Toronto, Ontario M6K 3E7
Canada

Cataloging in Publication Data is on file with the Library of Congress
ISBN: 1-58479-363-5

The text of this book was composed in Electra and Helvetica.
Printed in China

10 9 8 7 6 5 4 3 2 1
First Printing

Stewart, Tabori & Chang is a subsidiary of La Martinière Groupe

LA MARTINIÈRE
GROUPE